THE ART OF SHELLCRAFT

Also available in this series
Appliqué
The Art of Dried and Pressed Flowers
Bargello
Children's Clothes
Country Crafts
Filography: An Introduction to Thread Sculpture
Framing
Furniture Making
Gifts
Home Decoration
Jewellery
Macramé
More Soft Toys
Pottery
Rugmaking
Soft Toys
Weaving

THE ART OF SHELLCRAFT

Paula Critchley

PAN BOOKS LIMITED · LONDON & SYDNEY

First published 1975 by Ward Lock Ltd
This edition published 1976 by Pan Books Ltd,
Cavaye Place, London SW10 9PG
© Paula Critchley 1975

Design by Design Practitioners Ltd
Layout by Juanita Grout
Drawings by Paula Critchley
Photographs by Michael Lorenzini

Printed in Great Britain by Cripplegate Printing Co. Ltd., Edenbridge.

ISBN 0 330 24691 7

CONTENTS

INTRODUCTION

Most of us have a strong acquisitive urge, and there is no better way of satisfying it than to make a collection of sea-shells. Nearly everyone gets the chance of the occasional day's outing, or even a holiday by the sea, and the enjoyment of collecting lovely things for nothing, and probably in fine weather too, is a pleasure that few of us would want to miss.

Shells have fascinated people for literally thousands of years, and it is easy to see why. Very many are extraordinarily beautiful and have the most compelling shapes, textures, colours and patterns imaginable. They can vary in size from the minuscule – hardly visible – to the enormous Giant Clam, found in tropical reefs, which can measure up to $4\frac{1}{2}$ ft or 1·50 m long. Some shells are found so rarely that they become collectors' items; others are so profuse on sand or rocks that they completely cover whole stretches of the shore. The huge variety of different species – over 100,000 – to be found all over the world gives one some idea of the possible scope.

Apart from being lovely things just to collect and look at, shells have, and always have had, a great many uses – practical, ornamental, monetary and their contents are often, of course, edible. Their practical and ornamental uses often coincide, and include pearl buttons made from the Commercial Trochus, cutlery handles carved from the Golden Lip Pearl Oyster, inlay work made from thin layers cut from the Pearly Nautilus and cameos shaped from Bull Mouth Helmet Shells. Primitive societies often used shells to represent money, and indeed, Cowries are still used in this way by some tribes. As for the edible shellfish, certain species have become renowned in dishes such as Clam Chowder and Moules Marinière. The Oyster has always been regarded by connoisseurs of sea food as the most delicate. Using shells in a creative or practical way is taking the fun of collecting them one step further. The rewards are doubled: instead of having only a collection of shells in a box, they can be displayed in pictures, used as containers for plants, made into jewelry, used to decorate frames, and of course, provide the owner with an extremely interesting hobby. None of the techniques described in this book are at all complicated, and very little in the way of equipment is needed. For many items only adhesive is necessary – plus a little imagination. A child with reasonable dexterity could certainly cope with many of the ideas, and I have found that children particularly enjoy using shells which they have collected themselves.

Although it is not at all necessary to know anything about sh... ...te them, some basic information about them, such as their habitats, methods o. ...nd identification is essential in order to be able to plan proper shell-collecting exp... ...is, and make the most of the different beaches which are within easy travelling distance of home. Chapter 1 gives some fundamental help with these subjects, and some suggestions on how to clean and store the shells until you are ready to use them. Chapter 2 includes some general advice about using shells and is referred to throughout the book.

CHAPTER I
SHELLS AND
SHELL-COLLECTING

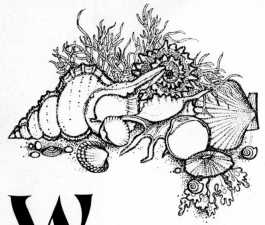

Whole volumes have been filled with information about the sea-shells of the world. This brief chapter merely aims to give enough help to increase your interest and pleasure in shell-collecting and enable you to make your own creations. Every aspect is explained as simply as possible; nevertheless a few words (for which there are no alternatives) may be unfamiliar to readers and for this reason a short glossary is included at the end of the chapter.

WHAT SHELLS ARE

Shells are, generally speaking, the protective homes of the invertebrate animals known as molluscs that live inside them, but not all molluscs have shells. For instance slugs, or shell-less snails, are molluscs and the group of marine molluscs known as Cephalopods (which include the Cuttlefish and the Squid) mostly have internal shells or none at all. The material which makes the shell is secreted by the mollusc itself when it is still very tiny. The substance is known as Conchiolin, and it is formed from calcium and other minerals which the mollusc extracts from its food. Conchiolin is liquid, but soon hardens on exposure to air or water. It is released by the mantle and the mantle's edge of the mollusc, and the final shape of the shell depends on the shape of each particular mantle edge.

CLASSES OF MOLLUSCS

There are over 100,000 species of mollusc known to exist in the world. About half this number live in the sea. As a group, only insects are more numerous. There are six classes of marine mollusc of which the Gastropods and the Bivalves, added together, are fifty times greater than the sum of the other four classes.

1   **Gastropods or Snails** *(Gastropoda).* This is the largest class, with about 80,000 different species. They are found in the sea, in fresh water and on land, and most of them have shells. These are always single, and very often coiled. Some simpler forms of Gastropods, like Limpets and Nerites, are not coiled, but this type is generally the exception. Non-marine species are very adaptable and can be found in the most extraordinary places like deserts and the tops of mountains; some are even able to jump! They have an enormous range of shapes, colours, textures and sizes.

There are about 100 **Families** including Conchs, Cones, True Limpets, Keyhole Limpets, Periwinkles, Top Shells, Abalones, Wentletraps, Turbans, Sundials and Ceriths (*see diagram A*).

Sub-species of just the True Limpet family number about 400 and include the Common Limpet, the China Limpet and the Spiked Limpet.

2   **Bivalves** *(Bivalvia).* These form the second largest class, and are known as *Pelecypoda* and *Lamellibranchia.* There are about 20,000 different species, most of them living in the sea, but some in fresh water. As their name implies, they have two valves joined by a hinge. Some bivalves stay in one place for most of their lives, others move around at a great rate, burrowing deep into the sand. Their shells are often more fragile than those of the Gastropods, and they are prey to carnivorous snails which bore holes through one of the valves near the beak in order to eat them.

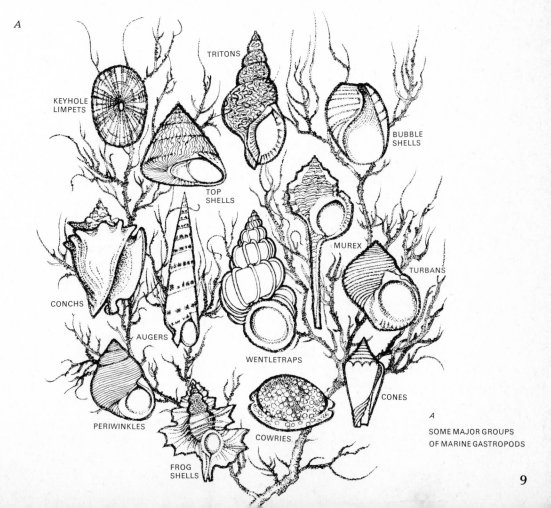

A

SOME MAJOR GROUPS
OF MARINE GASTROPODS

PIDDOCKS

THORNY OYSTERS

VENUS CLAMS

TELLINS

RAZOR SHELLS

ARK SHELLS

SCALLOPS

MUSSELS

COCKLES

WEDGE CLAMS

B

SOME MAJOR GROUPS OF MARINE BIVALVES

The Families include many edible types like Mussels, varieties of Oysters and Clams, Cockles and Scallops. Others, less familiar perhaps, are Ark Shells, Tellins, Pen Shells, Piddocks and Lucines (*see diagram B*).

Sub-species of the Scallop family are numerous, and have a world-wide distribution. They include the Lion's Paw, the Leopard Scallop and the Great Scallop.

3 **Cephalopods** *(Cephalopoda).* This family, numbering about 400 species, are the most advanced class of molluscs. They are exclusively marine, and are nearly all carnivorous. From the point of view of being a useful source of material for the shell-collector however, they have severe limitations: they are nearly all shell-less! There is one family – the Nautilus – however, which provides exceptions; the quite extraordinary Pearly Nautilus (also known as the Chambered Nautilus) has been the object of veneration to painters, writers and poets for centuries (*see photograph 1, showing a section*). A few others have internal 'shells' like the Cuttlefish, which is also known as the Cuttle-bone.

4 **Tusk Shells** *(Scaphopoda).* These molluscs have shells which live up to their name, many of them looking exactly like little elephants' tusks. There are about 200 marine species, and many of them live in shallow waters and under the sand. Their shells are like tubes – hollow throughout (*see photograph 2*).

5 **Chitons or Coat-of-Mail Shells** *(Loricata).* These marine molluscs, of which there are about 500 different species, look more like beetles than molluscs. The shells are in eight

separate sections, known as plates, which overlap and are joined together by a sort of muscular strap, known as a girdle. They can often be seen on rocks, although a few live in deep water (*see photograph 3*).

6 **Monoplacophora.** This tiny group is impossible to collect personally, since they all live in the deepest waters. In fact, they were only known through fossils until twenty or so years ago, when the first living specimens were found by scientists. They are the most primitive molluscs of all.

The shells in the colour photograph on *page 18* are identified by a key.

SOME INTERESTING PECULIARITIES

The Australian Trumpet Shell is the largest gastropod in the world; it can measure 2 ft (60 cm) long.

The Giant Clam is the largest bivalve in the world, and can reach lengths of $4\frac{1}{2}$ ft (1·50 m). It is incredibly heavy; each valve needs two strong men to carry it. It is found in the coral reefs of the Indo-Pacific region.

About a dozen **Cones** are very poisonous, and can even kill. The **Geography Cone** and the **Textile Cone** are particularly lethal. Both of these are found off the Australian coast and are now being specially caught to be used in experiments to find an anti-serum. On no account should an amateur try to collect these beautiful shells. They are nearly all found in the shallow waters in the Indo-Pacific Province (*see photographs 4a and 4b*).

The Dye Murex gives out a yellow liquid, which when treated, turns into a purple dye. It was used extensively BC to dye cloth, but was uneconomic in the extreme; hundreds were needed to produce enough colour to dye a piece the size of a handkerchief.

Carrier Shells are the original shell-collectors. In particular, the **Japanese Carrier Shell** has a weird assortment of small gastropods, bivalves and even stones permanently attached to its surface (*see photograph 5*).

Shipworms, often correctly described as 'dreaded', make tunnels in wood, from which they extract their energy and food. This diet of sawdust can lead to the eventual destruction

1

2

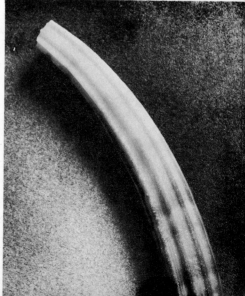

3

4a

5

4b

of ships, breakwaters; on one occasion it caused the total collapse of the Municipal Wharf House in Benicia, California.

Piddocks and **Date Mussels** make similar tunnels in hard clay and rocks.

The 'shell' of the **Paper Nautilus** is not really a shell at all; the female makes one as a sort of cradle for her eggs and discards it later (*see photograph 6 of the Nodose Paper Nautilus*). The byssus of the **Noble Pen Shell**, which is long and silky, was once used to make very fine cloth which was manufactured in Taranto, Italy.

Thorny Oysters are not in fact related to Oysters at all. They belong to the Scallop family. As a general rule, the quieter the water, the longer their spines grow (*see photograph 7*).

WHERE TO LOOK FOR SHELLS

Marine molluscs that live mainly on the shore, or in shallow waters off it, are the easiest for most collectors to find. Diving for shells is an occupation for trained people only, but it is a most exciting and rewarding way of collecting shells. Marine molluscs live in different locations according to the habitats and temperatures to which they are suited. In fact, water temperature is one of the deciding factors in the world-wide distribution of shells. As a general rule, those living in warm waters tend to be brightly coloured and marked, while those found in cold waters are not especially colourful. Accordingly, molluscs are found in the following regions:

The Littoral World is the world's coast-line, where molluscs live in sand and mud, in or on rocks, wooden structures, and in rock pools.

The Pelagic World is the area near the surface of the ocean where some molluscs live, hovering around or attaching themselves to floating seaweed.

The Continental Shelves and **Coral Reefs** stretch from low-tide mark to depths of about 600 ft (180 m) and many of the most beautiful species live here, where the waters are warm. The other oceanic regions are very deep, some reaching a depth of more than 6,400 ft (1,950 m).

Shingle beaches are the only unrewarding areas of the coast-line; no molluscs can survive being smashed against stones for very long.

Readers who would like to find out details about distribution in any particular place can do so through books and specialist journals, through the appropriate local authorities who, in my experience, are very helpful, through museums with natural history departments and through any of the world's numerous Shell Clubs and Conchological Societies. This general summary of what shells you are likely to find on what type of shore will give you some idea of what to expect.

Sandy shores are the habitats of many **Bivalves** although a few **Gastropods** do get washed ashore, but cannot live for long with nothing to cling on to. There will be lots of empty shells on the stretch of sand above high-water mark, which is known as the 'strand line'. It is likely that many of these will have been bleached by the sun, so it is a better idea to start your search just below the high-water mark and follow the tide out. Some species, when alive, just stay conveniently near the surface, or only half-buried in the sand. Others, like the Razor Shells, dig themselves in. You can usually tell where they are by small round depressions in the sand and they can be dug out with a small spade. Empty Piddocks can often be found. Look for Cockles, Tellins and Scallops (*see photograph 8*). Mussels mostly live on rocky shores, unless there are breakwaters or old wooden boats on the sand for them to cling to. Members of the Tusk Shell family can also be found here.

Rocky shores are often good hunting grounds with **Bivalves** and **Tusk Shells** living in the sand, and **Gastropods** and **Chitons** attaching themselves to rocks and living in rock crevices and rock pools. Gastropods like Limpets, Winkles, Top Shells, Whelks and Ormers will be found here, as well as some rock-clinging Bivalves like Mussels and Saddle Oysters (*see photograph 9*).

Muddy shores are really composed of a mixture of mud, sand and gravel. What sort of **Bivalves** you will find depends on whether mud or sand predominates, but look out for Gapers, Otter Shells, Hard-shell Clams and some Bubble Shells (*diagram C*). Take care that the mud isn't too squelchy; apart from being caked in it up to one's ankles, soft mud can be dangerous.

7

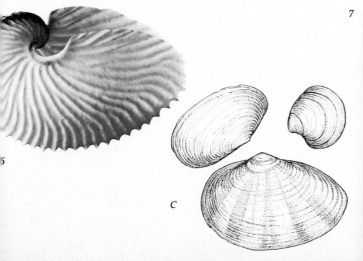

C

8   **Coral reefs** are the homes of some of the world's most outstanding shells. If you are lucky enough to be able to search for shells in these, expect to find colourful Cowries, Cones, Volutes, Conchs, Harps and Olives (*see photograph 10*).

Deep waters are the habitats of many molluscs that never get washed up on the shore. They have to be collected by deep-sea divers or dredged for by experts, and include the Precious Wentletrap, Spindle Tibia and Latiaxis Shells (*see photograph 11*). Amateur enthusiasts (with an experienced boatman) could certainly use this method in shallow waters of depths up to about 50 ft (15 m).

It is as well to know a little about tides, as much of the success of your expeditions will depend on careful timing. It would be very sad to arrive at a chosen beach, only to find that it was nearly high tide. Be very careful to leave a rocky beach or one backed by high cliffs well before high tide, as otherwise your route may be cut off by the sea.

TIDES

In order to be able to read Tidal Charts, it is necessary to understand what some of the terms mean. They are not at all difficult to master, but may be confusing if you have no previous knowledge.

Tides are influenced by the sun and the moon. The tides caused by the moon are twice as high as those of the sun, so in practice it is the moon that controls the tides. Both follow a monthly cycle.

The interval between successive **High Water** and **Low Water** is approximately 6 hours 13 minutes, and therefore between successive **High Waters** 12 hours 26 minutes. All written tidal information *is approximate* – so allow a good safety margin. The time of **High Water** comes, therefore, about 50 minutes later each day. In some parts of the world the height of tides can differ from the average. For instance, in Greece the tides are very small while those in the Bristol Channel are exceptionally high.

Spring Tides occur a little after both new and full moons – that is, about every two weeks. The height and range of the tide will be greater than usual. When the moon reaches its nearest point to earth, it is said to be in 'Perigee' and when this coincides with the time of the new or full moon the resulting Spring Tides are abnormally wide in range. The greatest tides of all occur near the **Equinoxes** (about 21 March and 23 September) when the night is equal in length to the day. These are the very best times to go collecting shells, as many more unusual ones can be found which are usually covered with water.

Neap Tides are smaller than average, and they occur half-way between each Spring Tide (a little after the first and last quarters of the moon). At these times the moon is farthest away from the earth and is said to be in 'Apogee'. These tides are not so useful from a shell-collector's point of view, as less of the shore is uncovered by water.

SHELL COLLECTING

1 ON THE SHORE If you are hoping to collect a great many shells at one time, you ought to think first about some form of transport. Shells can be surprisingly heavy, especially when caked with wet sand. You should remember that they may be too heavy to carry comfortably particularly if you have a steep climb from the beach, and for this reason a rucksack is ideal. Otherwise you need the following equipment:

strong plastic bags for putting the shells into, and perhaps one or two shallow boxes, preferably lined with cotton wool, in which to put very delicate shells;
a small spade, shovel or garden fork for digging out bivalves;
a kitchen knife with which to prise gastropods off rocks;
some small flat pieces of wood and fine string with which to secure chitons.

Chitons have to be placed flat immediately they are picked off the rocks, and tied in position, as otherwise they would just curl up into a ball.

A colander or basin is useful also for cleaning sand off the shells, but be careful not to dip it too far into the sea water, or the shells will all float away.

The same watchful eye needs to be kept on bivalves; the burrowing types will scuttle away again, unless you put them into a container immediately. For very enterprising people, who want to get rock-boring molluscs like Piddocks, be warned – a hammer and chisel are needed to break the rocks where they live in tunnels.

Look out also for smooth pebbles, Some beaches have coloured rock strata in pinks, yellows and greens and the resultant stones are very beautiful. Pieces of glass, worn smooth by the sea, driftwood, cork and seaweed can all be used in conjunction with shells for making pictures and murals.

2 DIVING FOR SHELLS This very rewarding occupation needs special equipment and training, otherwise diving is very dangerous indeed. Shallow diving – that is, up to a depth

11

10

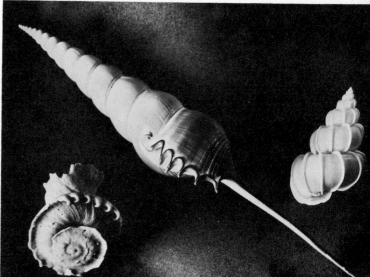

Opposite:
Equipment for the
shell collector should
include a strong
rucksack, bags
and boxes

of approximately 33 ft (10 m) – can be undertaken using an oxygen mask. At a greater depth, a proper diving suit and helmet has to be worn.

3 DREDGING FOR SHELLS This method is undertaken by both professionals and amateurs. The latter use home-made dredges, made usually of strong wire-mesh and reinforced with a strong material like steel. The most useful shape is rather like a large scoop. It is lowered into the water from a rowing boat to a depth of about 50 ft (15 m) by means of a rope, and dragged along the sandy bottom. If the capacity of the scoop is sufficiently large, it will be necessary to bring it to the surface by means of a winch.

4 BUYING SHELLS There are many species that you will not be able to collect for yourselves unfortunately. Most specialist shops will send you lists of current stocks, and you can usually order shells by mail. Some shops sell small bags of one variety; these can be very useful when you need 'background' colour.

CLEANING SHELLS

As soon as you get them home you will need to clean those shells that have living creatures in them. This can create problems if you are staying in an hotel, as you will need to boil them. However, the smell of decaying molluscs would probably force even the most unwilling staff into providing you with a pan and stove for ten minutes.

Put them into cold water first, and bring them slowly to the boil. This is the most humane method of killing them. Leave gastropods for a few minutes in the boiling water before taking them out and leaving them to cool, as it is far easier to extract them when they are cold. Bivalves are ready to be taken out of the water when their valves begin to open – the time varies according to their size, but about five minutes is the average. They can be cleaned straight away with a small, pointed knife or old nail file. Make sure that every bit of the mollusc is scraped away. If you want to keep some bivalves looking as if they were still closed, you can keep the two valves in position with an elastic band.

Gastropods are a little more tricky to clean, as the animals inside are coiled and can break off if not very carefully extracted. I find the best way of getting them out is to bend a pin into a semi-circular shape (a safety-pin is even better, as you can hold it by the head) and dig the point as far under the top of the mollusc as possible. Do not lift it straight up, as this might break it, making it difficult to get out the other bit, but just ease it slowly over the edge of the shell and it will come out in one piece.

For shells that are already empty, all you need do is to give them a good wash in warm water (with detergent if you like), and scrub off any dirt with an old toothbrush.

Shells that *should* be white but have got any seaweed stains on them, can be immersed in a household bleach solution for the recommended time. On no account use bleach on

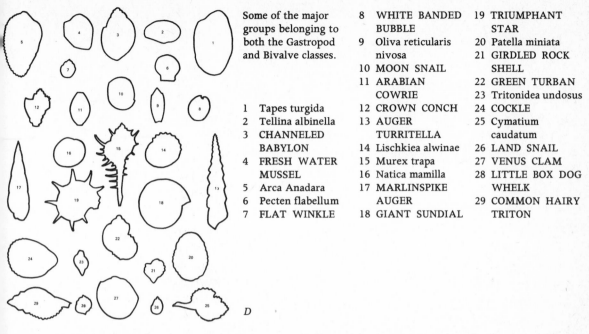

Some of the major groups belonging to both the Gastropod and Bivalve classes.

1 Tapes turgida
2 Tellina albinella
3 CHANNELED BABYLON
4 FRESH WATER MUSSEL
5 Arca Anadara
6 Pecten flabellum
7 FLAT WINKLE
8 WHITE BANDED BUBBLE
9 Oliva reticularis nivosa
10 MOON SNAIL
11 ARABIAN COWRIE
12 CROWN CONCH
13 AUGER TURRITELLA
14 Lischkiea alwinae
15 Murex trapa
16 Natica mamilla
17 MARLINSPIKE AUGER
18 GIANT SUNDIAL
19 TRIUMPHANT STAR
20 Patella miniata
21 GIRDLED ROCK SHELL
22 GREEN TURBAN
23 Tritonidea undosus
24 COCKLE
25 Cymatium caudatum
26 LAND SNAIL
27 VENUS CLAM
28 LITTLE BOX DOG WHELK
29 COMMON HAIRY TRITON

D

shells of any other colour. Black stains (tar and oil) and orange stains (rust) are too stubborn to be removed by anything; the best place for them is the rubbish bin.

IDENTIFYING SHELLS

When they are dry you will need to sort the shells out into Families before storing them. In this way, you will be able to find a particular shell easily when you need it. If you are quite knowledgeable about some of the sub-species, you will want to try and classify them in some detail. For beginners, a good handbook with plenty of coloured photographs and illustrations is probably the best way of getting to know and identify the main groups and the individual shells. Study the characteristics and shapes of each group of shells. Some of them are very easy to identify as they always follow a set pattern; Cowries, for example, are invariably smooth-topped and glossy and Slit Shells are instantly recognizable by the slit cut in the outer lip of their shells. Top Shells are always conical and Augers are long and slim with lots of whorls. Many well-known shells will be familiar to you already. All shells are known universally by their Latin names: for example the Papal Mitre would be *Mitra papalis* in Latin. The family name comes first, then the sub-species, followed very often by the name of the author who first named it; thus its full official name is *Mitra papalis Linné*. I have used the most familiar English names throughout the text and have given their Latin equivalents at the end of the book.

STORING SHELLS

Having classified your shells you will want to store them safely. If you have a varied collection, you will need the appropriate storage facilities. Use shallow flat-bottomed containers – chocolate boxes, matchboxes, lids, etc. It is wise to separate large and small shells of the same sub-species so as not to crush the smaller ones. This applies particularly to bivalves, which are generally more delicate. Very tiny ones should be kept in cotton wool. Grading shells for size, apart from ensuring them a long life, is a very necessary aid to finding the right ones when you start working with them. There is nothing so frustrating as scrabbling through a box full of shells, in order to find a particular size, and then breaking some of the others in the process. Grading for colour is also very useful for some species like Scallops. Very strong shells like Cowries could be kept in a glass jar until you need them; indeed, this is a decoration in itself.

When you label your shells, it is a good idea to add the name of the place where you found them and the date.

GLOSSARY

Aperture	*The opening of gastropod shells*
Beak	*The tip of a valve*
Byssus	*A bundle of silky threads attached to a few species like Pen Shells*
Class	*One of the six classifying groups: e.g. Gastropods*
Family	*Major types within each class: e.g. Fig Shells*
Hinge	*Where the two valves of a bivalve join*
Lip	*The rim of the aperture of gastropod shells*
Mantle	*Envelope of flesh enclosing a mollusc's inner parts, like skin*
Sub-species	*Particular types within each Family: e.g. Atlantic Fig Shell*
Whorl	*A single turn in a spiral shell*

BRITISH AND AMERICAN EQUIVALENTS

U.K.	*U.S.*
Blu-Tack	Plastitack
Card	Poster board; tagboard
Cow Gum	Elmer's or Sobo
Craft knife	X-Acto
Foam polystyrene	Styrofoam
Fabric adhesive	Duco cement
Frame kits	Frame kits generally made in metal, not wood
Hardboard	Masonite
Hessian	Burlap
Impact adhesive (Evo-Stik)	Impact adhesive
Paper adhesive	Cellular wallpaper paste
Pebbledash	Rockdash
Plasticine	Non-hardening oil-based modelling clay

BOOKS

SEASHELLS by S. Peter Dance, The Hamlyn Publishing Group Ltd, London, 1971.
SEASHELLS OF THE WORLD by R. Tucker Abbot, Ph.D, Golden Press, New York, 1962.
SEASHELLS OF THE WORLD WITH VALUES by A. Gordon Melvin, Charles Tuttle Co., Rutland and Tokyo, 1966.

CHAPTER 2
USING SHELLS

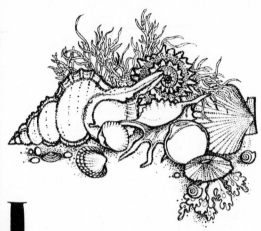

Like Ralph, who discovered the trumpet-like quality of the conch in Golding's *Lord of the Flies*, so have countless people, past and present, discovered the varied potential of shells. From jewelry and utensils to entire rooms and even houses, shells have been used creatively, sometimes with great artistry. Such creations have not all been the world of professional craftsmen. In 1739, for instance, the Duchess of Richmond and her two daughters started work on the Shell Pavilion at Goodwood Park, Sussex. It took many years to complete and is a most outstanding example of creativity allied to perseverance. There are often to be found small seaside cottages, the outside walls of which are completely encrusted with shells embedded in cement or allied to pebbledash; and the authorities in many seaside towns decorate public gardens with inlays of shells.

Although no complete beginner would be wise to embark on such ambitious projects straight away, the techniques described in the following chapters are applicable to small and large scale works alike. Thus, methods used for making pictures could well be used for walls; instructions for jewelry-making could be adapted to make mobiles; and suggestions for planting flowers in shells could be extended to create an entire shell garden either in or out of doors.

Types of Shell

You will find that the most useful shells to have in your collection are those of regular shape, whether round, oval, pointed, conical or oblong. These act as backgrounds to the main focal points, rather as a plain wall shows up pictures, and are invaluable for most of the projects described in this book. It will depend on the type of work that you are most interested in doing as to how large a quantity you will need of each species. Obviously you will need only a few for making jewelry, but far more for making a picture or a mirror frame. Some useful sorts to collect for this purpose are members of the following Families:

Augers, Bubble Shells, Olives, Lucines, Margin Shells, Nerites and Turritellas. The colour photograph on *page 35* shows seven species. Reading from just right of top-centre and working round clockwise, these are: Mussels, Banded Whelks, Limpets, Tellins, Top Shells, Cockles; and Periwinkles are in the centre.

The colours of shells are mostly very subtle and many are in shades of creamy white, pale pink, cream, beige and varying browns. A few shells, such as the Poached Egg Cowrie and the Little Egg Cowrie (both of which belong to the Egg Cowrie family) are pure white. There is no such thing as a black shell, though some are dark grey or have very dark grey markings, like the beautiful Marble Cone which has white triangles on a dark background. Some families provide very colourful shells – Scallops in particular can be yellow, pink, orange, red and mauve. The Lyrate Cockle is of such an unusually deep red for a shell that it looks almost as if it had been painted.

Considering the enormous variety of colourings and markings among the 100,000 known molluscs it is odd that three colours – blue, mauve and green – are so poorly represented. Many types of Mussel are of course blue; and some are even attractively striped in tones of blue. The pearly interiors of some shells have a bluish tinge and a few shells, such as the Festival Snail, have blue markings but it does not seem to be a popular colour. Mauve is not much better served – a few examples are found in the Scallops already mentioned, Violet Snails and the Purple Drupe, which is in fact purple only along its opening. Examples of shells which are green are the Green Turban, the Emerald Nerite and the lovely green operculum (the plate over the entrance to the shell) of the Tapestry Turban, known as the 'cat's eye'. Some shells are famous for their incredible and sometimes geometrical markings. Many members of the Cone Family, for instance, have patterns made up of zigzags, squares, spots, bands, triangles and scribbled lines. Some shells, such as members of the Harp Family, have both intricate markings and a sculptured, ribbed surface. Many shells have, indeed, very interesting surfaces; the Magnificent Wentletrap, pure white, has whorls delicately cross-hatched; the Rotary Star Shell has a spiralling frill and many Thorny Oysters have what their name suggests – 'thorns' or spikes. Ideally, a collection of shells with which to work should take into consideration four characteristics: (a) colour, (b) texture, (c) shape and (d) size. As far as sizes are concerned, shells measuring from about $\frac{3}{8}$ in (10 mm) to about 2 in (5 cm) will be the most useful for general purposes, with the obvious exception of large shells to be used as containers for plants.

Working with Shells

Shells can be fixed not only to each other but to wood, hardboard, cardboard, card, mounting board, plaster, metal, glass, mounts covered with canvas or heavy linen fabric – in fact to most strong, rigid surfaces. They can be embedded in cement or plaster – but never in clay, which shrinks as it dries out.

Many other items, particularly those with marine associations, such as coral, pebbles, driftwood, dried seaweed, seahorses and bits of glass worn smooth by the water can be used in conjunction with shells. Other bits and pieces that may come in handy and which you will probably have in the house anyway are wire in assorted thicknesses (useful for making 'stalks' for the flowers in shell pictures and as whiskers, antennae and so on for shell animals), beads and string (also for animals) and small items, perhaps of personal interest, to incorporate into shell jewelry.

Each chapter lists the essentials needed for each particular type of work. Strong adhesive, preferably of the kind known as epoxy resin, is common to nearly all the designs and is therefore the most necessary item to have – indeed, for making some shell animals it is the only thing you will need. Epoxy resin adhesives are made with two components, resin and hardener, which are mixed together in equal amounts to make an extremely strong adhesive which, when set, bonds two materials together inseparably. Adhesive must be used very carefully, applying just the right amount for each shell – too much and it will ooze out underneath; too little and it will not hold the shell. An orange stick or sharpened matchstick is a very good applicator; anything broader would be less accurate, particularly for very small shells and when making jewelry.

Sinking part of each shell into cement or plaster calls for a bit of practice; a good idea of the finished result should be in your mind before you start setting the shells as the cement itself is drying out all the time it is exposed to the air and if you work too slowly it may dry completely before the design is finished. Also, taking wrongly placed shells out of wet cement leaves an impression which may be difficult to eradicate. Start with something like an old earthenware plate which has only a small area for the cement to fill; and keep the design straightforward.

Some shells can be balanced either way up. This applies particularly to many bivalves, which have a convex and a concave side. Regularly shaped gastropods and Tusk shells can also be placed either way. Shells that are slim and pointed should, if used upright, have adhesive applied to their apertures and be supported by surrounding shells. They can also be fixed sideways. Some types of coral, unless quite small, are tricky to fix properly. Having lots of points and few flat surfaces makes it necessary to provide extra support from a shell or shells wedged around. Very large pieces of coral should be avoided, as generally they will take too little adhesive to ensure a sufficiently strong bond.

Different effects can be achieved by gluing the bases of suitable shells at an angle of 45° and supporting them in this position until they are firmly set. Alternatively, one shell can be placed in another with its apex resting over the edge; an example would be an Auger lying in a Costate Cockle. One shell will only balance on top of another if their two surfaces fit; it is no use trying to force them or they will look uneasy and will probably slide apart. It can be maddening to find the perfect shell to represent some animal's head, only to discover that in no way will it fit on to the perfect body.

Planning Designs

No book can teach people to design – that is to achieve an interesting arrangement of shapes and colours. There are no rules and each person will have individual likes and dislikes, tastes and imagination. However, I should like to make one plea – never paint or varnish your shells. They are beautiful in their own right and added colour or varnish ruins them. Even rather ordinary looking shells have characteristics that make them interesting and certainly worth preserving in their original form.

PICTURES   When trying out an arrangement for a picture you can approach the design in two different ways. Either you have a fixed idea of what you want to achieve – an all cream and pink design, for instance – or you let the shells dictate their own arrangement by moving them around until you become inspired and create a composition that satisfies you. Consider the shells in relation to their background colour, whether it be natural or painted; look out for clashing colours or tones and unpleasing colour combinations. There are no rules about these matters; two tones of the same colour may look right to one person and wrong to the next. It is generally thought that there is no such thing as a horrible colour in itself; colours only look unpleasant when two that 'kill' each other are put together. If you are painting a background or covering one with paper or fabric, colours associated with the natural habitats of shells, like sand and sea, would probably be preferable to using reds or purples unless you intend to use only white shells, which could look quite dramatic. Black and dark brown act as a foil to many shells and interesting effects can be achieved by using a background of the same colour as the shells to create an all-white or an all-yellow effect. If you want to make a pattern radiating from a central point, be sure to mark the centre in first, otherwise you may find the outer rings of your design disappearing off one edge of the picture. Make certain, too, that you have enough shells of each sort to be able to complete the design.

When you have decided on the preliminary basis of your arrangement it is best to glue the first shells down at once. If you wait until you have laid out an entire arrangement it will be very difficult to lift the shells out from the centre to fix them in position, without joggling others out of place. Some shells may also need supporting in particular positions until the adhesive is set, which means that you can only do a certain amount at a time anyway. Lumps of Blu-Tack are excellent propping-up devices, but if you do not have this material handy a good substitute is Plasticine. Pebbles or stones of the right size and weight can also act as props.

DECORATIVE FRAMES Mirrors, marine prints, old sepia photographs of beach scenes – any suitable picture can be framed with shells. Wooden frames of the right width can be made to measure, or old frames can often be bought cheaply. If the picture is a coloured one make sure that the surrounding shells complement it and are not too overpowering for the subject matter.

MAKING ANIMALS These are great fun to make, as many of the more usual types of shell like Cockles, Tellins, Slipper Shells, Mussels and Wedge Clams are already reminiscent of various animals' characteristics. Bivalves that have had holes drilled in them by carnivorous gastropods and shells worn into odd shapes by the waves; encrusted ones and those with marine growths attached to them, should be kept for this purpose. Do not start out with any preconceived ideas about *what* to make – if you do you will spend all day hunting round for appropriate shells to make a particular animal and very possibly end up with the body and legs but no head that will fit properly. It is best to be guided by the shapes of the shells themselves and how they fit together. You will soon find out what kind of animal you are making!

JEWELRY If you have a few shells which are both strong and attractive, making them into simple pieces of jewelry is an easy and rewarding hobby, particularly for beginners. Rings, for instance, can be made even by very young children. There are some shells which have a gem-like appearance, being smooth-surfaced, glossy and beautifully coloured or marked; many Moon Shells, Cowries, Cones, Volutes and Olives come into this category. Others rely for their interest on their sculpted surfaces; and, providing there are no long spikes to get caught or break off, shells like small Whelks, Ceriths and Turbans can be used to make pendants and necklaces.

DECORATING OBJECTS AND MAKING DECORATIVE ARTICLES Old clocks, wooden boxes, miniature chests-of-drawers – endless things can be given a new lease of life by applying shells to them. The designs should take into account the fact that the object you make is likely to be displayed in the home and will have to be moved for cleaning, so not too many sharp-edged shells should be used in case they get damaged. As is shown later, shells can be used not only to decorate various articles, but practical objects can be made out of the actual shells themselves.

SHELLS AS CONTAINERS – AND CONTAINERS FOR SHELLS Large shells with wide apertures make lovely containers for both living plants and permanent arrangements of dried flowers and leaves. A Triton Trumpet at least 6 in (15 cm) long, or any other appropriate shell which is deep enough to take roots or stalks, is ideal and makes an original alternative to the more usual flowerpot or vase. In reverse, as it were, shells themselves can be kept in transparent containers such as glass storage jars, which have lids or stoppers to prevent the contents becoming dusty. Such jars make unusual and charming decorations.

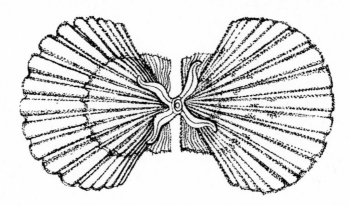

CHAPTER 3
THE PICTORIAL ASPECT

People generally seem to feel that a picture should be exactly as defined in the Oxford Dictionary – 'a representation of something produced on a surface by painting or other means' – in other words that a *real* picture is either painted or drawn on to a flat surface. Quite rightly, painting is taken very seriously – or serious paintings at least are taken seriously. But for many people the opportunity to learn to paint never occurs, or if it does they feel diffident about learning the techniques involved or, having learned them, about their ability to express themselves satisfactorily in the medium of paint. 'Other means' are any mark or marks made in any way on any suitable surface; or any objects, flat or raised, glued to or embedded in any appropriate background. Works of the latter kind are known as collages and shells are the ideal material to use for this purpose, coming as they do complete in themselves and needing no extra attention other than cleaning. Their shapes lend themselves to many different types of design and pattern.

Whatever sort of picture you want to make, the background must be strong enough to take the weight of the shells. Backgrounds for large pictures or those using particularly heavy shells, will need to be very rigid indeed; those for small pictures or ones using lighter shells need less rigidity. Decide first which type of picture you are aiming for and then choose your background accordingly.

BACKGROUNDS

Wood, hardboard and cardboard – left natural, painted or covered with strong fabric – are the most usual and inexpensive surfaces to work on. Natural wood, particularly pine with its interesting grain and knots, makes an attractive background for dark shells and also has the advantage of being thick enough to take picture screws, so that a frame is not essential, though the edges must be sandpapered to take off any roughness. The wood

surface can be sealed with two coats of clear polyurethane, which comes in two finishes – matt or gloss. A few woods, like some varieties of teak and rosewood, do not take kindly to being sealed, so check on the manufacturer's recommendations when buying your material. Wood can, of course, be painted with household paints.

Hardboard can be painted, too, either on the smooth or the textured side. It can also be bought in a sandy colour, very appropriate for shells, as well as in the more usual brown. Hardboard is strong enough to be used for large works, but cardboard or mounting board is not unless it is backed by hardboard or plywood. Both of these can be covered with a fabric that is closely woven, such as hessian (burlap), linen, strong cotton, gingham, canvas, velvet or felt. To get the fabric stretched really tightly over the hardboard or cardboard, it is best to sew the material firmly together at the back. Place the board on the wrong side of the material, making sure that the edges of the board are along the straight grain of the weave. Allow an extra 2 in (5 cm) of material all round the board (rule lines the appropriate distance away as a guide). Cut the material and, using strong thread, or very fine twine, sew the opposite edges of the material together, keeping the fabric as taut as possible (*figure Ea*). Repeat the process in the opposite direction, mitring the corners (*figure Eb*). As you sew, join the lengths of thread together with knots – this is much quicker than finishing off all the time as you only have to thread the needle again. Another method of covering is to glue the extra border to the backing, but it is more difficult to get the fabric stretched tightly enough if this way is used.

Using paper to cover a piece of cardboard or mounting board can present problems. Some papers – particularly if they are not very heavy – tend to buckle when glued to a large area. It is better to use ready-made coloured mounting board, bought from an art supplies shop, backed with hardboard or plywood. Some framers sell the cut-out centres of mounts quite cheaply. If you do decide to use paper, however, make sure that you use a suitable type of adhesive, such as Cow Gum.

Other good background materials are cork, glass, linoleum, formica and earthenware. However, as mentioned earlier, wet clay is unsuitable as it shrinks when drying out and anything embedded in it merely drops out. Expanded polystyrene or surfaces painted with cellulose paints are not suitable either as both are badly damaged by adhesives. I once made the mistake of using polystyrene as a background and found, some hours later, that the adhesive had eaten a hole right through it!

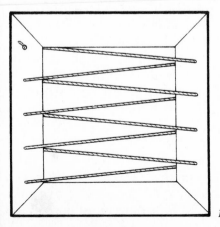

Ea

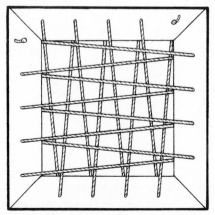

Eb

ADHESIVES

The type of adhesive that creates the strongest bond of all is *epoxy resin* such as Araldite, as already described. Slightly less powerful but still extremely strong is *impact adhesive*, such as Evo-Stik which, when first squeezed out of the tube or poured out of the tin is rather too runny to use successfully, but becomes 'tacky' after some minutes. At this stage objects adhere to each other readily without sliding about and there is less risk of leaving trails of glue running from shell to applicator or, worse still, over the background itself. However, if this should happen don't worry too much. Many manufacturers supply a special cleaning product to use with their own adhesives and it is worth finding out about this before starting work. As suggested, thin pieces of wood such as orange sticks or matchsticks make the most useful applicators. The head of the applicator becomes thickened with adhesive fairly quickly, so it is best not to start with anything too broad.

FRAMES

Pictures can be made specially to fit old frames, or new frames can be made professionally or even by an amateur with a flair for carpentry and the necessary equipment. It is quite a tricky process, however, as success depends on cutting the four angles of the frame with complete accuracy so that they will fit together perfectly. Another solution is to buy a frame-making kit, which is cheaper than having a frame made professionally. The kits are easy to assemble, but do have the disadvantage of only being available in a limited range of sizes, so the frame should be bought before starting on the picture – or alternatively a note should be made of the sizes available in the required style. A plain slab of wood need not be framed at all if it is thick enough to have picture screws fixed to the back.

WORKING WITH CEMENT

Shells are often embedded in cement or cement mixtures to cover entire walls, whole rooms or even houses. Some cement mixtures can be tinted by mixing with ordinary powder or poster-paints; others need special cement pigments and manufacturers' advice should be obtained about what to use with what. As cement dries fast, designs should be worked out beforehand so that they can be put into position quickly. If the area to be covered is large, lay on the cement with a spatula or trowel, but do not attempt to cover too much at once. When the shell is in position it should not be taken out again or the surface will be left uneven.

A very good way of accustoming oneself to the use of cement is to start by using it on a very small surface, such as an unglazed earthenware plate (*see photograph 18*). Do not use glazed earthenware or china, otherwise when the cement dries it will just lift out in a flat disc, which may look interesting but will very soon break.

COMPOSITION

The arrangement of several components to make a pleasing whole in a given area is something that takes a little practice. There are no rules to observe, as in perspective drawing for example, but certain ideas come off while others do not. The most important ingredient

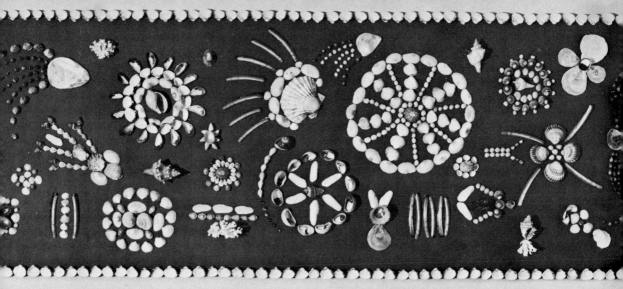

in any design is having a very positive idea of what you want to achieve, some point of 12 view that you want to express creatively. The old tag: 'Every pictures tells a story' does not mean that every picture should be illustrative, but that it should be personal. Inspiration can come from something seen, music heard – even from a particular situation or behaviour pattern. Posters frequently use very simple designs done in an abstract or symbolic manner to hammer home their message. The four children who made the large picture (*photograph 12*) frequently told me that they had some particular thing in mind as they worked out their seemingly random patterns. An exception to this, of course, is found in display pictures of special shells, where the important thing is to achieve a balanced effect.

Having said that there are no rules in composition – or that if there are they are there to be broken – it must be admitted that there are one or two types of arrangement that can look very uneasy. Pictures that have small arrangements towards the edges and nothing much going on in the centre lead the eye to nowhere in particular and give the feeling that parts of the composition are being pushed out of the frame. When spacing is used between shells or groupings of shells, this should be as interesting as the arrangements themselves.

MAKING PICTURES

When you have got a fairly good idea of what sort of picture you want to do and have chosen your background, get your preliminary arrangement right before gluing anything into position. Shells that you want to balance on top of each other can be kept in place temporarily with bits of Blu-Tack. Those to be kept in semi-upright positions, like the Cockles in *photograph 15*, can also be wedged and large, fairly flat shells can act as platforms on which to build taller arrangements. If the edges of a shell are a little chipped a light sandpapering will make them more regular, but never use any badly damaged shell unless you are satisfied that its shape is still attractive. Some that have been worn into weird shapes by the sea, or bivalves with holes drilled in them by gastropods, are often interesting but there is no point in keeping any shells with rust, slime or tar stains or any which have had the apex broken off.

Once you have arranged a small area as you want it, glue the shells down before the picture gets too crowded as the presence of a number of shells makes manœuvring more difficult. Also, if too many are arranged before you start gluing them, or if the work has to be left for any reason, there is a likelihood that the shells will get jogged out of position. Before lifting each shell to glue it mark its place with something small, like a pin, to make sure of re-positioning correctly.

Most strong adhesives take at least twelve hours to set hard and epoxy resins do not reach their final stage of firmness for three days. You can hasten the process a little if the work is left to dry in a warm place.

Pictures made on a velvet background attract particles of dust, which can easily be removed by dabbing with the sticky side of a length of Sellotape or Scotch Tape. Velvet should be protected by glass and for work of this type you really need a box type of frame with deep sides. Velvet has the advantage, shared with fabrics like felt and hessian, of a slightly rough surface which prevents the shells from sliding about while they are being arranged. If you intend to frame a picture be sure that you leave a margin of about $\frac{3}{4}$ in (19 mm) all round your design. If for any reason this is impossible the picture can be mounted on a piece of hardboard, cut a little larger all round so as to fit the frame. Fix the picture screws in the frame before finally fitting the picture as otherwise it will be difficult to exert enough pressure on the back to screw in the eyes without crushing the shells. For the same reason panel pins to hold the back of the picture in place should be half inserted beforehand and then bent down over the back of the mount when the picture has been fixed.

1 CHILDREN'S MURAL *(5 ft 6 in × 2 ft; 1.65 m × 60 cm)*. Four children from my class, all aged eleven, who were free at the beginning of the summer holidays, volunteered to combine their efforts to make a group picture, which is shown on *page 29*. All four were used to working in each other's company but only two, who were twins, had actually worked together on a similar project. Having agreed on what form the mural would take the twins prepared the wood and painted it with household paint. Then they started work with the other two, one at each corner, to produce these attractive random patterns. Many of the shells used were collected by them and me on the coast; they include Slipper Shells, Top Shells, Piddocks, Whelks, Mussels, Periwinkles, Cockles, Tellins, Razor Shells, Clams, Oysters and Scallops. They also used Mitres, Tun Shells, Fig Shells, Margin Shells, Vase Shells, Tulip Shells, Rock Shells, Chanks and pieces of Coral. The mural was completed with a border of Cockle Shells, concave side up.

2 DISPLAY PICTURE OF MINIATURE SHELLS *(8 × 6 in; 20 × 15 cm)*. This picture, shown in colour, in *photograph 13* and *diagram F*, demonstrates a good way of using small shells, if you have only one or two specimens of each type. This collection was arranged on a dark, marbled paper which had been mounted on to very stiff card. The patterns on the background are reminiscent of the seashore but are subdued enough in colour to show up the shells well. To achieve a balanced effect, try using a few larger shells to offset the smaller ones (the smallest measures less than $\frac{1}{2}$ in or 6 mm) and some coloured, marked or textured ones to offset the pale shells.

3 DOOR ORNAMENT *(3 ft 2 in × 4 in; 96 × 10 cm)*. This design, shown in colour and in *photograph 14*, was made to fit over the top of a door. A cuttle-bone – the internal shell of the Cuttlefish – forms the centre of the piece, surmounted by a knobbly Cerith and Piddocks complete with marine growths. These are flanked by Helmet Shells, Mussels, Wedge Clams, Nerites, Cockles, Scallops, Turritellas, Augers, Olives, Periwinkles and Top Shells. The background is a pine plank, given two coats of sandy yellow household paint; the design is based on a bird's outstretched wings. During the making many shells, tilted

Miniature Shells

1 TELLIN	10 Bullia	18 DOVE SHELL	26 PERIWINKLE	39 UNSTABLE
2 TURRITELLA	11 JOB'S TEAR	19 PAINTED TOP	27 NETTED DOG	LIMPET

1 TELLIN
2 TURRITELLA
3 PERIWINKLE
4 TELLIN
5 ROCK SHELL
6 VENUS CLAM
7 LAND SNAIL
8 COMB SHELL
9 KEYHOLE
 LIMPET

10 Bullia
11 JOB'S TEAR
12 PHEASANT
 SHELL
13 LYNX COWRIE
14 CONE
15 Tectarius
 muricatus
16 CERITH
17 WANDERING
 COWRIE

18 DOVE SHELL
19 PAINTED TOP
 SHELL
20 KEYHOLE
 LIMPET
21 OLIVE
22 DOVE SHELL
23 MUREX
24 NUCLEUS
 COWRIE
25 PELICAN'S FOOT

26 PERIWINKLE
27 NETTED DOG
 WHELK
28 COCKLE
29 OLIVE
30 TOP SHELL
31 LUCINE
32 EUROPEAN
 COWRIE
33 PERIWINKLE
34 COMB SHELL
35 WEDGE SHELL
36 BANDED WHELK
37 TUSK SHELL
38 ATLANTIC
 BUBBLE SHELL

39 UNSTABLE
 LIMPET
40 COMMON
 MUSSEL
41 ZEBRA ARK
 SHELL
42 TELLIN
43 SCREW SHELL
44 LAND SNAIL
45 EUROPEAN
 COWRIE
46 CHINAMAN'S
 HAT
47 ROUGH WINKLE
48 ARK SHELL
49 CHINA LIMPET

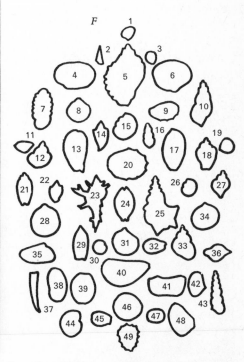

at angles of 45°, had to be supported on either side by the shells on which they rested. Others were propped up with Blu-Tack.

4 STEERING-WHEEL PICTURE *(24 × 24 in; 60 × 60 cm)*. A formal, round design like this one, based on a ship's wheel and shown in colour and in *photograph 15*, suits a square frame. The background is dark brown hessian or burlap, sewn over a hardboard mount as shown in *diagrams Ea* and *Eb* and the picture was made in its frame. First of all the centre was found by stretching two lengths of string from corner to corner, to find where they crossed. This central point was marked with white crayon. Then a pair of compasses was used to draw the large outside circle, adding the inner circles as the work progressed towards the middle. Almost the entire design was carried out with Cockles, both convex and concave side up, with the addition of Pearly Trochuses, dark grey Scallops, pale yellow Money Cowries, an Owl Limpet in the centre and a Scallop at the top.

14 5   ABSTRACT PICTURE   *(22 × 30 in; 55 × 75 cm)*. This composition of shells, pebbles, dried seaweed and coral, shown in colour and in *photograph 16* is also carried out on a hessian or burlap background incorporating favourite specimens, like the Star Shell, Harp, the large white Giant Cockle, Auger Turritellas, a Snipe's Bill Murex and a Costate Cockle. The latter had a slightly broken valve, which the overhanging piece of agate managed to disguise. The pebbles are smooth, beautifully coloured and marked, some with quartz. Pieces of sea-worn glass, of which there is one in the picture, slate, sea-fans (which are made by Coral Snails) and in fact anything interesting that you pick up, could find a place in this type of picture.

6   FLOWER PICTURE   *(12 × 11 in; 30 × 27·5 cm)*. The background of this picture, shown in *photograph 17*, is a heavy, sandy-brown paper mounted on board. When making pictures representing anything as small as buds, petals or wings you will certainly need a pair of

15

16

17

Opposite:
Seven useful species:
clockwise from top
right, Mussels,
Banded Whelks,
Limpets, Tellins, Top
Shells, Cockles,
Periwinkles in
the centre

Overleaf left:
Simple, but varied
equipment needed
for Shellwork

Overleaf right:
Three very differently
designed types of
picture, with an
unusual and
decorative door
ornament

Following page:
An abstract picture,
mounted on dark
brown fabric, which
includes pebbles and
seaweed as well
as shells

fine tweezers with which to pick up the miniature shells. You will also need some pliable wire, like the garden wire which was used here, if you want to imitate stalks. These should be glued to the background before adding the shells that make the flower petals, as otherwise it is difficult to manœuvre the wire between the finished flowers. The butterflies' wings are all made of different species of Tellins, with Ceriths, Augers and Turritellas forming the bodies and Tusk Shells, Squilla Claws and fine wire used for the antennae. The small butterfly sitting on a stone had been made for a different project (it is shown in *photograph 23* in Chapter 5) but it fitted perfectly into this scheme, both in colour and size. Bits of coral and little Mussels were used for leaves, Money Cowries, Jingle Shells and Rose Petal Tellins for flowers. European Cowries, looking like pebbles themselves, are placed next to real pebbles at the base of the picture. Any tiny shells can look like buds or flower centres; those in the picture include Limpets, pink Top Shells and Chink Shells.

7   DECORATIVE PLATE   *(6 in or 15 cm diameter)*. For this project, shown in *photograph 18*, cement mixture for indoor use was mixed with sufficient black poster or powder paint to turn it into battleship grey and a layer about $\frac{1}{4}$ in (6 mm) thick was used to coat an unglazed earthenware saucer. A delicate white Top Shell in the centre is flanked by small Tellins and Dove Shells (of the Pyrene family). Four pairs of Mantle Scallops, attractively marked in tones of dark red, form the second ring; and Common Cockles interspersed with more Dove Shells complete the circle.

18

CHAPTER 4
FRAMED

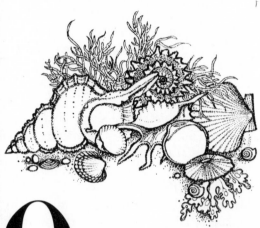

Old photographs and picture postcards are seldom considered worthy for mounting and framing, but they can be made to look very attractive surrounded by simple arrangements of shells. Oil paintings are perhaps the exception, but otherwise almost any picture, such as the prints, old playbills, decorative maps and so on frequently to be found among the paraphernalia of junk shops and attics, can be given a similar new look. Creating a shell frame for a piece of mirror glass is an effective way of producing something that is out of the ordinary, costs a fraction of the store price and gives you the added satisfaction of having made it yourself. Nor is it always necessary to use conventional frames for pictures or mirrors; two of the examples here have no frame at all (*photographs 20* and *21*) and are simply mounted on to wood which has been covered with fabric. This method has the great advantage over framing that you do not have to buy or make a new frame, nor are you confined to the particular measurements of an old frame which may not be the size you require. However, if you do want to use an old frame that is really too big for your purpose, a mount or background can be made to fill in the space between frame and subject, leaving plenty of room for the shell decoration (*photograph 22*).

There are, in all, five different methods of framing or presenting a picture:

(1) To have a special frame made
(2) To use a ready-prepared frame 'kit'
(3) To use an existing old frame
(4) To make your own frame
(5) To mount the subject on an unframed piece of wood.

Frames

1 Having a special frame made is the simplest and really the most satisfactory way of all, but unfortunately it is not cheap and in addition there is often a delay of some weeks

between placing the order and collecting the finished frame. However, the large selection of styles available, together with the benefit of the framer's expertise, will make it a worthwhile project for many people.

2   Using a frame kit provides the answer for people who do not want to have a picture framed professionally, but who want a professional finish all the same. In the United Kingdom most frame kits are sold in packs of two sides – either two widths or two heights – so that two complete packs are needed to make one frame and variations in the finished size of the frame are not difficult to achieve. As a general rule the shortest lengths you can buy are about 10 in (25 cm) and the longest about 3 ft (90 cm), while the intermediate measurements go up by about 2 in (5 cm) at a time. The kits are completely ready to assemble and come with instructions that are very easy to follow – all that is needed is a strong adhesive.

3   Using an existing old frame, providing that it is not falling to bits, has a lot of advantages over newer frames – one of them being that frames aren't made like that any more! It is practically impossible to order round, oval or hand-carved frames now. If you have no suitable old frame and want to buy one cheaply, look in junk shops, antique markets, jumble sales and auction sales. You will probably have to buy the decrepit pastel drawing or stained watercolour that goes with the frame, but it should still not cost much. The warm colouring and soft, mottled markings of maple frames make them well worth hunting for, though it is harder now to find them at bargain prices as they have become fashionable. Old wooden frames that have been varnished or painted can be stripped, like the frame shown in the colour photograph, using a special liquid stripper, and can then be repainted or left natural. Gilt frames that are in good condition should merely be cleaned with a dry cloth. Never use water or detergent as this rubs the gilt off. If a frame has already lost a lot of gilt or gold leaf it can be smartened up considerably with an application of either liquid or wax gilt, which is obtainable in most art supplies shops.

4   Making your own frame is not difficult if you have a certain amount of experience in woodworking and have access to the necessary tools, such as a saw, mitre-block, clamps and so on. Lengths of suitable framing can generally be found in art supplies shops, framers or home-handicraft stores. However, the process is a fairly intricate one, involving meticulous measuring and extreme accuracy, so should not be undertaken unless you are confident that you know what you are doing or are prepared to learn from your mistakes! Precise instructions for frame-making can be found in most books of do-it-yourself woodwork projects.

5   Mounting on wood is an alternative to conventional framing. Some types of wood, like pine with its interesting knots and grains, can be left uncovered, but functional wood such as chipboard can be covered with material, perhaps to complement or match an existing colour scheme. For either method you will need wood at least $\frac{1}{2}$ in (13 mm) thick, picture screws and picture wire. If you are covering with fabric you will need in addition a sufficient yardage of fabric with a firm weave, such as repp, cotton, hessian (burlap), velvet, felt or linen; pencil; scissors; tailor's thread or button thread; a sewing needle, cardboard or hardboard; a craft knife (X-Acto) and strong adhesive.

Have your wood cut to the required size and then cut the cardboard or hardboard slightly smaller – it will be used for backing the wood later. A craft knife will cut cardboard but you will have to saw the hardboard. Place your fabric right side downwards on a flat

surface and lay the wood on top of it, keeping the edge of the wood in line with the straight weave of the fabric. Draw round the area of the wood. Now measure the thickness of the wood, add an allowance of $1\frac{1}{2}$ to 2 in (3 to 5 cm) for sewing over the back and rule a second line the appropriate distance outside the first. Cut out the fabric and follow the instructions given in Chapter 3 for covering the wood with the fabric. When you have done this, glue the cardboard or hardboard backing over your stitching, weight it and leave it to dry. When it is thoroughly dry fix the picture screws through the backing into the wood. For both covered and uncovered wood, determine the exact position of the picture or mirror to be framed and then fix this in the usual way with strong adhesive, weighting it down until dry. If you are using a picture printed on thin paper it must be mounted on card first, as it is impossible to get thin paper to adhere satisfactorily to fabric.

Mirrors

WHITE MIRROR *(15 in or 37·5 cm square)*. This is shown in the colour photograph and also in detail in *photograph 19*. A plain wood frame was made and given two coats of white household paint. A square of mirror-glass was cut by a glazier to fit the recess (known as the rebate or rabbet) under the inner edge of the frame. The mirror was fitted into the frame and the back of it, with the upright sides of the rebate, spread liberally with glue. A piece of hardboard, cut the same size as the mirror, was placed on top and weighted for forty-eight hours while the adhesive set completely. The picture screws were then inserted and the mirror was ready for the shell work to begin. As it is all too easy to dribble glue on to the mirror while working, cut a piece of card to cover the area before you start fixing the shells.

I wanted to achieve an almost all-white look, occasionally relieved by touches of dark grey, beige, pink and brown. Among the white or nearly white shells were various species of Scallops, Prickly Frogshells, Common and Costate Cockles and Tellins. Dark grey Scallops,

Blood Cowries, Necklace Shells, Lady's Ears (members of the Moon Snail family), Augers, Turritellas, a Land Snail and a Vibex Bonnet provide the subtle colours.

MIRROR ON A FABRIC BACKGROUND *(14 × 16 in; 35 × 40 cm)*. A piece of chipboard was covered with heavy repp, as described earlier in this chapter, and backed with hardboard. The design round the mirror, shown in *photograph 20*, had to be carefully worked out first to make sure that there were enough shells of each sort needed to complete the geometrical pattern. Those edging the mirror are known as Coffee Beans and these shells are also found forming lines elsewhere; the white, rounded shells in two different sizes are species of the Tellin family; those forming a sort of rabbit's-ear pattern are Olives. In each corner is a small Mushroom Coral surrounded by tiny Cowries and Dove Shells with a single Turritella. The mirror is completed by two very familiar species – Limpets and Trochuses.

Pictures

H. C. S. MACQUEEN *(14 × 18 in; 35 × 45 cm)*. This lovely picture of an old sailing ship, shown in the colour photograph, needed a rather understated treatment to match its soft colouring. The honey tones of the sails, clouds and waves are echoed in the blond pine frame and many of the shells surrounding it. The frame originally had a badly damaged and chipped maple veneer, some of which peeled off easily while the rest needed to be helped off with a kitchen knife. The surface underneath was tacky with adhesive, but this came off quite easily when rubbed with a rag and turpentine. Finally a fine grade of sandpaper smoothed and buffed the wood until it looked almost like new. The frame was edged

22

with very small, sandy-coloured Cockles placed convex side up. In keeping with their pale tones are Piddocks, various Olives and Turritellas, an Owl Limpet and a Keyhole Limpet, with Moon Snails and Periwinkles providing the golden tones.

TWO LITTLE GIRLS *(9 × 7 in; 22·5 × 17·5 cm)*. This delightful postcard-size photograph of two children, shown in colour and in *photograph 21* was another junk shop find, unearthed from a pile of seaside views, bathing belles and nineteenth-century actors. The background is heavy pink cotton, with a plywood backing and a hinged plywood support. The photograph is edged with a double row of Cockles so small that they had to be picked up and placed with the help of tweezers. With the exception of the four pale blue Cowries with beige markings and the brilliant white Moon Snail all the other shells used are very ordinary, familiar ones – Piddocks, Margin Shells, Wedge Clams, Scallops, Limpets, Olives and Turritellas.

EDWARDIAN LADY *(20 × 17 in; 50 × 42·5 cm)*. This photograph of a great aunt, dressed in turn-of-the-century finery shown both in colour and in *photograph 22* was unearthed recently from a box full of family photographs. The sepia tones of old-fashioned studio poses have great charm, as does the model – sitting bolt upright, presumably because of her corsets! The maple frame was fortunately in good repair when it was found in a junk shop. The mount was covered in beige cotton and backed by hardboard to stiffen it. The swirling patterns are made from Coffee Beans (Margin Shells), Trochuses, Tusk Shells, Augers and Mushroom Coral. The Calico Clam at the top has a land Snail in it and at the base a Jingle Shell is surmounted by a pond Snail, then a Turrid and lastly a pure white Scallop.

CHAPTER 5
THE ANIMAL
KINGDOM

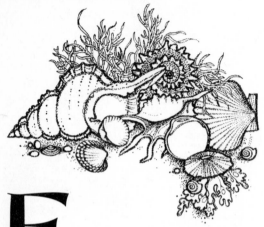

Fishes, animals and insects are described here and of all the designs in this book they are the most economical to make. Common marine shells, found on practically every seashore, are more useful in this context than the more exotic ones. The simple, regular shapes of Cockles, Tellins, Limpets and Mussels can represent heads, ears, bodies and tails better than shells which have more complicated or irregular shapes. As the animals are made on a small scale – the baby owls in *photograph 28* measure less than 1 in (25 mm) – it is a good idea when next making a visit to the sea to pick up some miniature shells if you do not have plenty already.

Auger Shells and Turritellas in different sizes and colours are not common in every part of the world, but they are most useful for making insects' and fishes' bodies, as shown in *photographs 24, 25* and *26*. Cowries also make well balanced bodies as seen in *photograph 33* and Periwinkles in all sizes can be useful for heads, eyes and paws as in *photographs 25* and *32*.

You will need the minimum of equipment. Strong adhesive – either epoxy resin or an impact adhesive – and some Blu-Tack are the only essentials. Small amounts of Blu-Tack are sometimes necessary, as already explained, to support shells in position while the adhesive is setting. It is also very useful as a temporary holding device when trying out designs. You will probably already have the other bits and pieces mentioned later in this chapter, like beads, wire and string and, as generally only very small amounts of adhesive are needed, the ever-useful orange stick or matchstick. Two things are very important to remember when trying out designs. Firstly: if it does not fit naturally and easily, never try to force one shell into or on to another; secondly: do not put too heavy a shell on top of another, nor try to balance a shell at an impossible angle. If you do, the whole structure will topple over.

The descriptions that follow should be regarded primarily as guides to the kind of effect

that can be achieved with different shells; alternatives have been suggested whenever possible.

INSECTS

Some bivalves, when opened, are like insects' wings in shape and often in colour, too. Those with semi-transparent or pearly interiors are particularly appropriate to use although they can, of course, be used either side uppermost. Marine invertebrates can make some quite realistic flying invertebrates!

When storing your shells try to keep some bivalves hinged together; not only are they very useful for this particular purpose, but they will suggest other uses, some of which are discussed later in this chapter. If possible keep them in a container wide enough for them to lie in one layer only; if they are piled up one on top of another some will break as you hunt through for just the right ones for your current project.

Insects on a larger scale can be made using Venus Clams, Oysters or Surf Clams, all of which are effective used either way up.

A few species of the gastropod class can also be used, but the scope is more limited and it may be difficult to team them up together. However, Limpets, particularly those with pearly or strongly patterned interiors, look very effective. This class does provide a wide variety from which to choose shells to represent insects' bodies: Augers and Turritellas,

23

with their slim coils, are the perfect choice. Other shells with long rectangular shapes are some members of the Turrid and Cerith families, Cones and Olives.

Butterfly on Stone

Small winged insects made out of shells, like the one shown in *photograph 23*, need something to balance on, as the wings are usually not stuck on to the body but on to a base. This flat-bottomed stone, dark grey streaked with white, makes a good contrast to the pale pink and white Rose Petal Tellins. The body is a tiny Cerith, measuring only $\frac{1}{2}$ in (13 mm) and it is stuck down with the aperture uppermost. The wings are made of miniature Rose Petal Tellins; the two top ones are twice the size of the bottom pair. The antennae are single strands of unravelled picture wire, the kinks ironed out with scissor blades and then slightly curved between finger and thumb. A good way to fix them in place is to dip the ends in the adhesive, slip them in place just under the 'head' or aperture and support them with little pellets of Blu-Tack or Plasticine while they are drying. If the ends are not of equal length, snip them level when the adhesive has hardened.

Three Butterflies on Driftwood

Pieces of driftwood make good perches for shell insects and the small bit of sea-worn bark in *photograph 24* has crevices into which the butterflies' bodies fit. A pair of pink Tellins are placed each side in the hollows. A shiny brown Auger forms the body and two Squilla Claws (from the Mantis Shrimp) make the antennae.

24

The two smaller butterflies are made with pairs of hinged Tellins and Wedge Clams. The one that is almost closed at the top has two tiny Olive Shells (known as Rice Shells) one either end, representing its body; the bottom one has a Cerith body and the same picture-wire antennae as described for the single butterfly on the stone. As they are placed at angles they should be propped up with Blu-Tack or Plasticine until set.

Two Dragonflies

Again, very common shells are used for the two dragonflies in *photograph 25*. For the bodies I chose two smooth, white Turritellas of slightly different sizes and placed them facing each other on a piece of slate. Other shells in other colours would, of course, be just as appropriate. If you have not collected enough double Mussel Shells to make the wings, use single ones of the same size that can be paired together. A good way to fix the wings in a semi-upright position is to dip the very end of each Mussel (separated from its double) into the adhesive, slip it into position under the body and support it with Blu-Tack to prevent it from slipping down while it is setting.

When the adhesive is dry add a head to each body. I used yellow Periwinkles. Antennae can be made from any fine wire, or from pins like the black and white glass-headed ones used here. Again, I suggest that you dip the ends of the pins or wire into the adhesive and fix them in the same way as the wings.

FISH

Fish are probably easier to make than any other creatures. Their basic shapes are simple and sometimes just the addition of two bulging eyes can turn the well-chosen shell into a fish. The addition of fins, either in pairs to represent the pectoral or pelvic fins, or singly

to look like the tail fin, can add authenticity. The apertures of some shells when seen longitudinally look uncannily like fishes' mouths when open. Children find these rewarding to make as they can use their imagination about shapes and have fun adding the details.

Flying Fish

It has just hit the water – the water being a flat, silvery stone. The body of the flying fish shown in *photograph 26* is a light brown Auger shell with white markings, called a Dimidiate Auger; its wing-fins are the separated halves of a Heart Cockle on which the eyes – minute Periwinkles – are placed. A bright orange Scallop forms the tail. A young pupil worked this one out, holding the parts together temporarily with Blu-Tack until she had an arrangement that suited her. Then she used adhesive in the usual way to fasten them.

Swimming Fish

Often shells with very neat holes bored by predatory snails are found on the shore; such a one is the Venus Clam used for the gaping fish in *photograph 27*. It might equally well have provided the basis for a bird, with a beak pushed through the hole. Squilla Claws formed the pectoral fins at the sides and the dorsal fin on its back. Rose Petal Tellins, white uppermost, were used for the eyes.

BIRDS

The view from my workroom window is of a park-keeper's lodge where several fan-tail pigeons live in the garden. Their house gave me the idea of making a similar one to display shell birds. The pigeons are replaced by a family of owls, however, as being more practicable for me to make with the types of shell I had. Instructions for making the owls' house are given later in this section.

Family of Owls

The group of seven owls in the colour photograph and *photograph 28* consists of three little ones, two middle-sized ones and two large ones; the largest measures under 2 in (5 cm), so the scale is very small. All their bodies are made from Top Shells, which are conical. There are over a thousand species to be found all over the world and many are delicately beaded in concentric whorls. Owing to the slight unevenness of their apertures, Top Shells tend to lean a little to one side. A bit of Blu-Tack strategically placed underneath will balance them and will also keep them in place on whatever surface you choose to put them. Ordinary Common Cockles of appropriate sizes are used for the heads, with the beak of the shell forming the beak of the owl. The apex of the Top Shell is pointed, so in order to give

28 a bed for the Cockles to sit on I used a little Blu-Tack instead of adhesive to position the heads. The eyes were drawn with a pen and black ink. As an alternative to Cockles try using Tellins of a rounded variety, which also have a pronounced beak.

The wings are pairs of Wedge Clams. To stop them from sliding down when glued to the Top Shell they should be supported with Blu-Tack.

The Owl House

I made the house shown in the colour photograph using natural clay, which is a lovely material to work with and quite durable once it has been fired.

NATURAL CLAY can generally be bought in art supply shops by weight; this is far more economical than buying it pre-packed. It is very heavy and the house in the photograph took about 9 lb (4 kg) of clay to make.

Natural clay is a moist, malleable material and to prevent it drying out it must be kept in a strong, airtight container when it is not being used. Only take out enough for your immediate needs and sprinkle the clay model with a little water from time to time. Between modelling sessions keep your work covered with a plastic bag, the inside of which is slightly wet.

However, only comparatively few people have access to a kiln for firing models made of natural clay – and if such models are not fired they will be extremely fragile. But for the beginner there are now some very satisfactory modelling materials available which do not have to be fired. Among these is *Newclay*, which is most suitable for fairly large articles. It consists of grey clay to which fine nylon fibres have been added for strength and to prevent warping and cracking as the work dries out. After it is dry the work can be further strengthened by using a special hardener made by the same manufacturers. Newclay needs to be kept damp during modelling in exactly the same way as natural clay.

Modelling with clay or Newclay
There is no need at all to buy expensive modelling tools; slim-bladed knives, small sharpened sticks, even an old screwdriver, will all be just as useful. Your hands will do most of the work anyhow.
The Owl House was modelled on a wooden board so that it could be turned in any direction for working purposes. A solid, four-sided shape was roughly built up, taking care to press each lump of clay down well, so as not to leave air bubbles inside. This is important as air bubbles will weaken the model and will cause it to distort or crack. The angle of the roof was then shaped and, before any doorways or decorations were considered, the basic shape was hollowed out. This prevents the cracking which takes place when too solid a lump of clay is fired. The walls and roof should be left about 1 in (25 mm) thick.

With a small knife shape doorways and windows; add windowsills and any extra decorations you like, such as tiles for the roof or shutters for the windows. All additional pieces must be firmly fixed, using a little water to moisten them and create a bond between them and the body of clay, as otherwise they are likely to fall off as they dry.

Leave the model to dry out completely in a room with a warm, even temperature – never in a cold, damp place. The drying times will vary according to size and to the clay you have used. When Newclay is completely dry, use three or four coats of hardener on it. Natural clay, when dry, is ready for firing followed by glazing or painting. Newclay can be painted with emulsion paint tinted with powder colour and given a final coat of Newclay Gloss for a shiny surface.

Fan-tail Pigeon

Like the shell with its ready-made hole suggesting an open mouth, which was used to make the swimming fish, so can shells worn into odd shapes by the sea, suggest ideas. The mis-shapen mollusc in the colour photograph and *photograph 29* was once an Oyster; its indented tail and puffed-out chest, however, strongly suggested a bird. A Tellin, complete with a grey beak, was the perfect head and two tiny black beads made the eyes. Beads are very difficult to pick up, glue and put in just the right place, so the best way to go about it is to find a darning needle that is too thick actually to go through the bead but which will hold it in position. Add a dab of adhesive to the bead and place it, still on the end of the needle, on to the shell; then gently push if off the needle, using finger and thumb.

When the body, head and eyes are set, the legs can be added. I used two broken-off pieces of coral. Place a fair quantity of adhesive inside the shell on either side, in order to make a firm surround to hold the legs in place and take the weight of the whole bird. Stand the bird on its tail in a lump of Blu-Tack while the coral sets.

ANIMALS

The animals in this section were all made because individual shells had strongly suggested a particular animal's face or, like the mouse and vole, face and body.

The Mouse

Those shells that resemble beaks, as described earlier in the section on birds, can also look like animals' noses. The mouse in the colour photograph and *photograph 30*, which is easy to make, uses a Cockle, oval in shape, for its body and head. The ridges on the shell even seem to suggest whiskers. The ears were formed of two tiny Cockles (Tellins would be an alternative) held in place by small pieces of Blu-Tack while the adhesive was setting. The rest was even simpler. Two small beads for eyes; two paws made out of dark brown paper and a thin piece of string for a tail and the little animal was complete.

The Rabbit

Those rather dull molluscs, Slipper Shells, proved invaluable for making the rabbit shown in colour and in *photograph 31*. The pointed end of the shell, slightly askew, looked very like a twitching nose. I found two very small Slipper Shells to make the ears and used a pink Top Shell for the body. The rabbit's feet, placed close together, are Tellins, flat side

down; and its tail is a Job's Tear, a member of the Wedge Clam family. Yellow beads were added for eyes while the whiskers are four short strands of coarse string fastened together with a few twists of fine wire and stuck to the underside of the Slipper Shell. Pieces of fine wire or bristles from a brush would do just as well.

Vole at Home

A shell with a pointed apex, when its breadth is not excessive, will often fit into a wide-apertured gastropod, making a creature and its home in one move, so to speak. Examples of the former type of shell are numerous and include Turritellas, Ceriths, Augers, Mitres and Volutes. There is also a wide choice of shells to consider as the 'home', including Turban Shells, Tun Shells, Murex Shells and Rock Shells.

For the Vole in *photograph 32* I added Periwinkle paws, partly to fill the gap between the Cerith body and the Turban home and also to suggest rodent characteristics. Small black beads for eyes, mounted on the bases of minute Tellins, complete the little creature.

Opposite:
A white-framed mirror
decorated with shells,
nearly all white, but
with touchés of grey,
beige, pink and brown

Overleaf left:
A honey-coloured
pine frame delicately
edged with shells,
echoes the colours of
an old picture

Overleaf right:
An old sepia
photograph is shown
off by the warm pink
background; the
foreground shows
many ways of using
shells of all sizes

31

Opposite:
Miniature birds and
animals make up the
crew of this small ship

32

33

The Frog and the Donkey

Pairs of open shells sometimes seem to have ready-made facial expressions, suggesting the appearance of various animals.

THE FROG shown in colour and in *photograph 33* is as simple to make as the Mouse, described earlier. Hinged Tellins were used for the head, which was fixed at a slight angle on to an orange Moon Snail. Disproportionately large wooden beads made the eyes and the webbed feet are claws cut off a paper bird that once decorated a Christmas tree – these could equally well have been cut from paper. The head, glued only at the beak of the bivalve, shakes up and down in an amusing way.

THE DONKEY in *photograph 33* has a double Mussel as its half-open mouth, which gives it immediate character. Wedge Clams made the ears and a generous amount of adhesive was used to fix the head and ears to the body, for which I used a large Mouse Cowrie. When these were set, more Wedge Clams were used to make the hooves and haunches. The tail was made from a short length of coarse string, the end of which was fluffed out and wired to prevent it from fraying further. Scotch tape may be used to stop fraying at the other end. The tail was stuck in the radula (the serrated groove in the base of the Cowrie) and left to set. Finally a few snippets of dried seaweed formed the mane and the forelock.

CHAPTER 6
SHELL JEWELRY

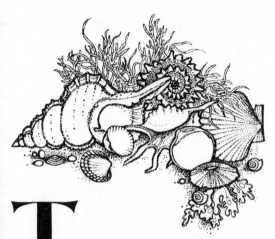

The tradition of shell jewelry goes back thousands of years. Archaeologists have found shell necklaces buried with ornaments and utensils that are 30,000 years old. The islanders of the Pacific and Indian Oceans thread small shells to make bracelets, necklaces and pendants; primitive tribes once used necklaces of this sort instead of money. Cowries, in fact, are still used as currency in some places today. Bangles made from sections cut from Chank Shells are worn mainly by Hindu women in Bengal. These are sometimes elaborately carved and coloured, with inset jewels, and used as marriage bangles.

Cameo cutting was practised by the ancient Babylonians and Phoenicians, and reached the height of fashion in Victorian times. Italy – and in particular, Florence – is famous for cameos, using either onyx or different types of Helmet Shell. The inner shell layer forms the background to the cameo, varying from light red to deep brown according to the species used.

Nineteenth-century craftsmen used shells and mother-of-pearl extensively – no museum of Victoriana is complete without its glass-domed sprays of shell flowers and its mother-of-pearl inlaid papier-mâché work.

Ordinary pearl buttons are made from the Australian Top Shell, and often show traces of colour on the backs; buttons with a grey pearl appearance are cut from the Black Lip Pearl Oyster of the Indo-Pacific.

Pearls, themselves some of the most beautiful of jewels, beloved and coveted through the centuries, are found in pearl Oysters; fresh water Mussels can also yield very fine specimens. Although some shells are very rare and therefore very valuable like the Glory-of-the-Sea Cone and the Leucodon Cowrie – only five specimens of which are known to exist – many are there just for the picking. Even if you have to buy some they can be of the cheaper varieties. Nearly all shells are attractive in their own right, and many different types can be used for making jewelry. Some specialist shops sell bags of shells all of one type – a very good way of buying a lot of useful material for very little money indeed.

The bracelets, rings, ear-rings, brooches and pendants photographed in this chapter are specially designed for beginners and children to make. Getting a professional-looking result is relatively easy and quick, particularly when using just one shell on a mount.

TYPES OF SHELL TO USE

As jewelry is to adorn a person, or a person's clothes, the materials used must be as strong as possible. Rings, in particular, are liable to get damaged more easily than brooches, and should be made from shells that have no fragile parts to break off. For this reason it is generally best to use gastropods although certain species of bivalves have almost unbreakable edges and are equally strong (see photograph 34). A tough bivalve like the Gold Lip Pearl Oyster used as a pendant in photograph 42 is almost as strong as a Cowrie. Some fragile shells can certainly be used in shell jewelry provided they are protected inside

34

35

something else, like the little Mussel shell inside the Spiny Cockle brooch (see photograph 38) or like the Rose Petal Tellins surrounded by Augers in the star-shaped brooch (see photograph 39). Almost all shells are beautiful for their colouring, markings, textures or shapes and brown Nerites (see photograph 37) can be just as interesting to use as the topaz-coloured Moon Snail used for the ring (see photograph 35).

EQUIPMENT

The equipment needed to turn your shells into pieces of jewelry can be kept to the minimum. A pair of jewelry pliers, some tweezers, adhesive, some kitchen salt or Blu-Tack and the appropriate mounts are all that are necessary to begin with. Of this short list, only the pliers are relatively expensive compared with the other items.

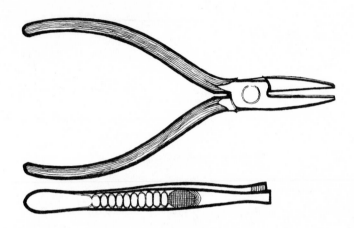

Pliers *(see diagram G)*
Small pliers are used to prise open jump rings from which to hang shells, to bend the 'claws' of claw ring mounts, to press bell caps on to shells, and to make copper wire pliable. If you have two pairs, one can be used instead of tweezers to grip the metal while the other pair does the work. The flat-ended variety is the most useful to have.

Tweezers *(see diagram G)*
Two pairs of tweezers are ideal; a pair of flat-ended ones to use in conjunction with pliers, and a pair of fine pointed ones which are useful for picking up very small shells and holding them in position while the adhesive is applied.

Adhesive
The adhesive used must be of a type that sets extremely hard and is suitable for metal, china, glass, wood as well as for setting shells on to mounts. Epoxy resin adhesives, of which there are many brands, are ideal. Provided they are used according to the manufacturer's instructions, and are left to set for at least 12 hours (preferably in a dry, warm place) they will bond one surface to another permanently. Use an old saucer or something similar for mixing the adhesive and the hardener but never use a plastic surface – the adhesive will eat a hole in it. As recommended earlier, use a sharpened matchstick or orange stick for applying the adhesive to the surface; the area to be glued is generally rather small, and an applicator with a broad end is less accurate to work with. Some adhesives have tackier consistencies than others. Those that are more 'syrupy' when first squeezed or poured out should be exposed to the air for five minutes or so to become 'tacky' before use. A much better bond is then achieved and the shells are less likely to slide out of position. The right amount of adhesive must be carefully calculated: too much, and it will

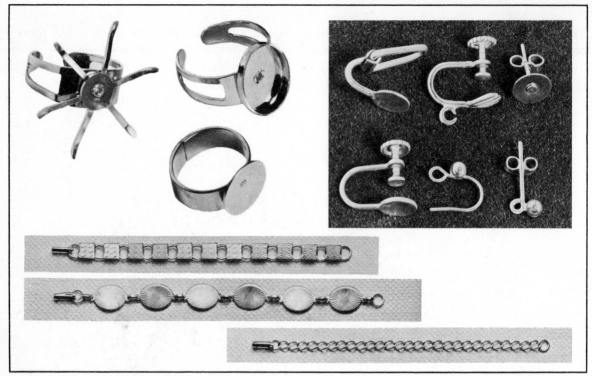

spread out from underneath and show; too little and a heavy shell will part company from its mounting.

Salt-pots or Blu-Tack *(see diagram I)*
Shells, once mounted, need a firm resting place to keep them upright while they are setting. There are two ways to achieve this. Either fill a pot with about 1 in (2·5 cm) of kitchen salt and rest the mounted shells in that or use Blu-Tack as a 'bed'.

Mountings
All the mountings described here can be bought from specialist shops and are usually made in copper, or have 'gold' or 'silver' finishes.

BROOCH MOUNTINGS *(see diagram H)*. These are generally of the flat pad type, and can be square, oblong, round or oval. Some types have a small rim, like a tray, which is filled with small shells. Small flat brooch mountings can also be bought for gluing to a plain mount or even to an individual shell.

RING MOUNTINGS *(see photograph above)*. Most of these are made to be adapted to any size of finger, and the ends can be made narrower or wider by squeezing them together or pushing them apart. The mountings themselves generally come in three varieties: a flat pad, a 'claw' fitting and one with indentations to take individual small shells.

EAR-RING MOUNTINGS *(see photograph above)*. These are made either with a flat base on which to mount the shell, or with a small ring from which the shell hangs to make drop ear-rings. Ear-rings are made for both pierced and unpierced ears.

BRACELET MOUNTINGS *(see photograph above)*. There is a wide variety from which to choose. Some are chain links and can have shells hung from them; some are flat pads, linked together, on which to glue shells. Others are broad bands of metal, often with a disc-shaped mounting in the centre. Bracelets can also be made by linking shells together with bell caps (*see photograph page 75*) and adding a fastening device.

BELL CAPS *(see diagram H)*. The aptly named bell caps are used for mounting shells to make drop ear-rings, pendants, 'charm' bracelets and so on. They are made in different sizes and shapes, with either 'gold' or 'silver' finishes and the prongs are pre-shaped with pliers or tweezers before adding adhesive and mounting on to the shell. Another type is a single patterned shape which has to be bent over and is useful for mounting flat-surfaced shells.

JUMP RINGS *(see diagram H)*. These rings are used to connect mounted shells when they

H

I

Opposite:
The owl family are
shown here outside
their own house

Overleaf left:
Shell jewelry –
brooches, bracelets,
ear-rings, necklaces –
are easy to make and
most effective

Overleaf right:
Shells, however small,
make, perfect
containers for
fresh flowers

are being used as pendants, ear-rings or necklaces. They can also be used as linking devices for bracelets. They are opened with pliers, slipped through the corresponding rings on both mountings, and then closed again with the pliers.

MISCELLANEOUS MOUNTINGS   Mountings are also available for making buttons, key-rings, tie clips and cuff-links (*see diagram H*).

Pieces of shell jewelry can be made using both ready-made mountings and less conventional methods. Beginners may like to make a simple ring first, and then progress to making more inventive and individual pieces.

The following designs are described only to explain the various necessary techniques. You will have your own ideas about what shells to use, and how you want to use them.

RINGS

To make successful rings choose strong shells the shapes of which do not interfere with the natural movements of the fingers. The shells should have flat, broad bases, so that they can balance properly on the mountings.

A RING MADE FROM A TOP SHELL   (*see colour photograph and photograph 34*). This very simple ring was made from a single Top Shell and a ring mounting with a flat pad. Put the ring mounting on your finger, then move the shell around on it to find the best position for setting. When you have decided on this, note where the bottom of the shell touches the mounting and put a little adhesive on it, and also on the pad of the mounting. Apply one to the other and leave in the salt pot or Blu-Tack to dry.

B RING MADE FROM A CARDITA   (*see colour photograph and photograph 34*). This ring is made in exactly the same way as the method described for the Top Shell. The Broad-ribbed Cardita is found in great numbers off the Florida coast and is a suitably strong bivalve to use for this purpose. A polished bit of Rose Quartz, pale and transparent, was placed in the centre, and then it was left to set in the usual way.

C RING MADE FROM A MOON SNAIL   (*see colour photograph and photograph 35*). Another way to make a ring is to set a shell in a claw mounting. The shell you choose should be regular in shape and have a smooth top surface. First, work the claws of the mounting with your pliers to make them more supple and then put the ring on your finger and see which way the shell looks best. When you have decided, take the mounting off and work the claws one by one round the shell, using the pliers. Before bending the claws finally into place, put a small dab of adhesive between the bottom of the shell and the mounting to make it quite firm.

Opposite:
Some shells are large
enough to hold small
houseplants, cacti
or succulents

EAR-RINGS

There are several types of mounting available for pendant, clip and screw ear-rings. The technique for making clip or screw ear-rings is exactly the same as for making rings on flat pad mountings. Pendant ear-rings are hung from their mountings by bell caps; sometimes jump rings are added.

Although no one gastropod is exactly the same as the next one, care should be taken when choosing a pair of shells to match them up as far as possible for colour and size.

36

37

PENDANT EAR-RINGS *(see colour photograph and photograph 36).* The points of these Olivancillaria shells fitted into these very small bell caps, without the caps having to be pre-shaped. Be careful to see that the little rings at the tops of the bell caps are positioned in such a way that the shells hang correctly from your ears when they are fixed on to the mountings. When you have decided on the best way of hanging them, stick a bell cap on to each shell, and leave to dry completely before attaching them to the ear-ring mountings you have chosen.

BUTTONS

The technique is exactly the same as that used for rings and clip ear-rings; a single shell is fixed to the flat surface of the button base. As buttons have to be got in and out of button-holes, choose shells that are smooth-topped and have no jagged edges. This limits the field a bit, but Cowries, Margin Shells, Top Shells and Nerites could all be used.

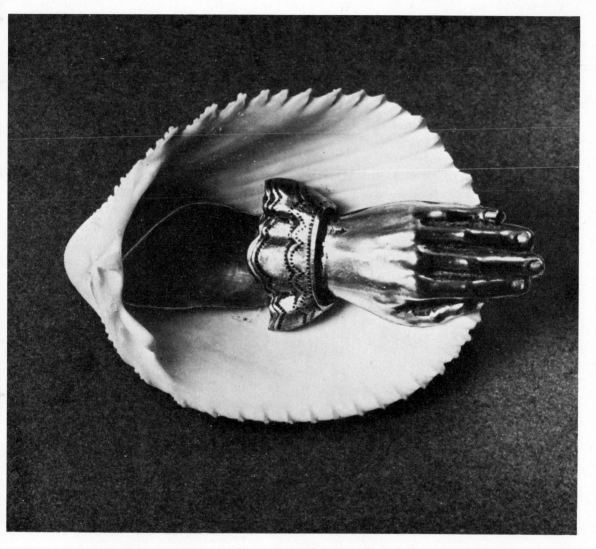

BUTTONS MADE FROM NERITES *(see colour photograph and photograph 37)*. The number of buttons you can make is limited by the number of matching shells that you can find. The shells must have bases broad enough to cover the button mountings. When you have chosen your shells, use a little adhesive to stick each one to its mounting, making sure that the shanks all face the same way (either towards the apex or the lip of the shell). Leave them, mounting side up, in a salt-pot until they are set.

BROOCHES

A good deal more artistic licence can be taken when you are making brooches. Firstly, they can be made on quite a large scale and incorporate several shells; secondly, they are more protected from knocks than rings are. All the same, it's advisable not to use fragile shells except when they are *either* inside a strong shell *or* set directly on to a flat surface next to a tall, stronger shell.

A BROOCH MADE FROM A SPINY COCKLE *(see colour photograph and photograph 38).* The brass hand, with its sleeve made out of a Mussel, makes an unconventional interior to this Spiny Cockle brooch. There is no reason why shells cannot be used in conjunction with any materials you like, providing they have an adequate surface to glue, are durable and look interesting. The delicate Mussel is placed out of harm's way, protected by the height of the sides of the large shell. A small brooch mounting, complete with pin, was moulded with pliers to the shape of the back of the Cockle and then fixed in place with adhesive.

B STAR-SHAPED BROOCH *(see colour photograph and photograph 39).* The basis of this rather Celtic-looking brooch is a copper disc 2 in (5 cm) in diameter. Clean the mount with a gentle scouring powder as copper attracts grease and any dirt on the surface prevents the adhesive holding properly. Turritellas were used to make the star, broad bases to the centre and points radiating outwards to project beyond the edges of the mounting. These shells were glued in place to form a bed for the central Limpet shell, yellow interior uppermost, in which was housed a marmalade-coloured Periwinkle. When these shells were completely set, adhesive was applied to the sections between the Turritellas, gluing one section at a time. Each section was covered with six very small Rose Petal Tellins set convex

39

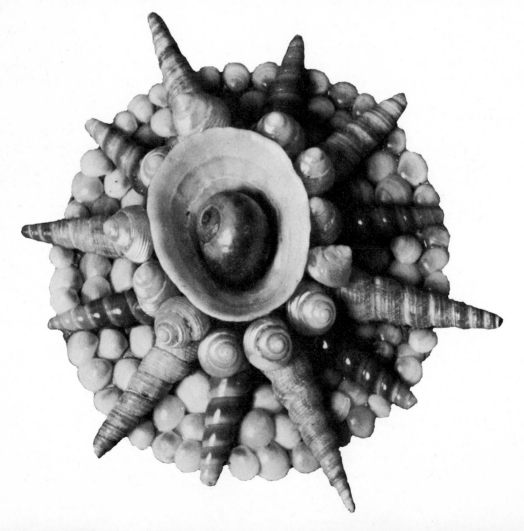

side up. As these shells are so tiny, it is best to pick up and place them with tweezers. *41* Pearly Trochus shells covered the bases of the Turritellas and completed the design. When the shells were set a small brooch mounting was glued under the copper disc, making sure that the pin was angled horizontally to the design, and the brooch was left shell side down in the salt to set.

BRACELETS

Two different ways of making bracelets are photographed and described in this chapter. Many other types can be made which need not use the conventional methods of mounting described at the beginning of this chapter. Leather bases could be used instead of metal or shells could be threaded together like those for the shell chain (*see photograph 42*).

A CHARM BRACELET *(see colour photograph and photograph 40).* A charm bracelet depends for its success on the careful choice of shells. These should be strong ones, of course, and can be different in kind as long as they are of similar size and colouring. The shells used here are, from left to right: (1) Cerith, (2) Clam, (3) Keyhole Limpet, (4) Cowrie, (5) Dog Whelk, (6) Scallop, (7) Bullia Whelk. Lay the bracelet chain straight and place the shells along it, moving them around until you have found a pleasing order and making sure that the best faces of the shells are all in the same direction without any overlap once they are hung. Mould a bell cap to fit the top of each shell, apply a little adhesive to cap and shell and press together. Leave the shells upright in salt until the adhesive has set. Fix two jump rings to each shell and count out the links of the bracelet chain so that the shells will hang at even distances from each other. Fasten the jump rings firmly with pliers.

B COWRIE BRACELET *(see photograph 41).* A linked bracelet can be made using only bell caps, connecting jump rings and a fastening device. Five Thrush Cowries were chosen to make this bracelet – their flat bases lie easily on the wrist. Take two bell caps for each shell and shape them to fit, one at either end. Fix them on with a small amount of adhesive, making sure that the ring of each bell cap is positioned so that the connecting jump rings will lie flat. Leave each mounted shell to dry on a *flat* surface, connect with jump rings and add a fastener between the two end shells.

NECKLACES

There are numerous ways of making necklaces which can take the form of a single pendant, several shells hanging from a chain, a 'collar', a chain made of shells and so on. Necklaces made of pierced shells have been made for thousands of years.

A SHELL CHAIN WITH PENDANT *(see colour photograph and photograph 42)*. A large Gold Lip Pearl Oyster makes the pendant for this necklace of Pearly Trochus shells. You will need some strong sewing thread but do not use nylon thread as it tends to stretch; a needle, a very fine skewer or a pair of compasses and a light hammer.

First pierce the Trochus shells so that they can be threaded. The easiest way to do this is to balance each shell on a wooden board, allowing it to rest naturally with the aperture facing upwards. Put the point of the skewer or compasses in the opening and tap gently with the hammer to pierce; you will feel the point go through. Be prepared for some breakages – you are unlikely to have one hundred per cent success. I used the shells in the proportion of five natural ones to one coloured. Cut the thread the length you want the necklace to be, plus about 6 in (15 cm) for finishing off and tie a knot a few inches from one end, making it large enough to prevent the first shell from falling off. Thread five natural shells, then one coloured, and so on – or use only natural ones. You will find that when you have strung several groups and pushed them along the thread, they will bunch up together. Make the chain long enough to go easily over your head, leaving a fairly long end of thread for finishing off.

Using the finest available hand drill, drill a hole near the top of a large shell such as the Gold Lip Pearl Oyster used here. Push the long end thread of the chain through the hole and pick up a Pearly Trochus shell, pushing it down so that it sits in the apex of the large shell and covers the hole in it. Work the thread back through the hole in the large shell,

42

44

thread it into a needle and stitch firmly through the starting knot until very securely
fastened. Cut off the thread ends.

B HEARTLOCKET *(see colour photograph and photograph 43).* The Heart Cockle, unusually hinged down the centre, is the perfect shape for a locket. As it is a bivalve, the
divided halves must first be joined together with a little adhesive and left to dry before
using. Then add a small bell cap, preferably of a simple type, and leave this to set as well
before adding a jump ring.

C NECKLACE WITH STAR LIMPET *(see colour photograph and photograph 44).* A heavy
chain needs a more positive treatment than the kind of fine chain described above.
The method of fixing, however, is the same; bell caps and jump rings are used, and the
shells are spaced in very much the same way as described for the bracelet on *page 75*.
The central shell, beautiful shown either way round, is a Star Limpet, and it is flanked by
Club Urchin Spines (not shells of course), and Dog Whelks.

CHAPTER 7
SHELLS AND FLOWERS

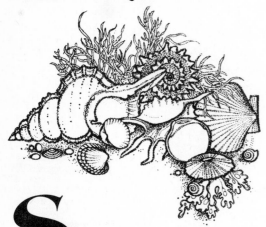

Some shells are wide enough, or have deep enough apertures, to make perfect containers for plants and flower arrangements. They look lovely in or out of doors; grouped on a windowsill; as a centrepiece for a table; among pots and tubs on a patio or decorating the corners of steps or low brick walls. Specimens of the largest shell in the world, the Giant Clam, which can measure over a yard – a metre or more – across, are sometimes used for fountains and no-so-miniature gardens, but are more likely to be found in a stately home than in a cottage garden. *Photograph 48* shows a small relation, the Fluted Giant Clam or Furbelow Clam, both valves filled with fresh flowers. This particular shell, measuring 8 in (20 cm) across, has inside one valve a non-precious pearl the size and shape of a broad bean.

The larger shells of the world come mostly from warm waters, which is unfortunate for shell collectors living in Great Britain and other areas in the Boreal Province (the Gulf of St Lawrence to Cape Cod; the south coast of Ireland; Norway; the Shetlands and Faroes and the Baltic). Shells like Cockles, Mussels and Winkles are characteristic of these regions and you cannot put much into a Winkle! However, medium-sized shells like Dog Whelks, American Whelk-tingles and the Atlantic Deep Sea Scallop, which can grow up to 8 in (20 cm) are quite common and although not big enough to plant in they could certainly be used for small displays of fresh or dried flowers. Specialist shops now offer so many fine shells often costing much less than conventional vases and containers and looking much more attractive, as shown in *photographs 45, 46* and *47*. Some readers may already live in or visit places where large shells can be found, or may be able to persuade friends or relatives to bring them back one or two from their travels. There are some beautiful large shells, such as the Queen Conch, King Helmet and the huge Green Turban to be found in the Caribbean.

Whatever your geographical circumstances, this short list of some of the larger shells of

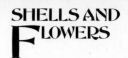
Previous page:
Small wooden boxes –
and even an old
wooden egg-cup – can
be decorated with
carefully matched
shells

Opposite:
This old clock, found
in a junk-shop, has
been transformed with
shells and tiny
pearl buttons

...he world, together with descriptions, maximum sizes and locations, may be helpful when
collecting or buying – or when asking other people to collect or buy for you.

Group	Sub-species	Description	Maximum Size	Regions
GASTROPODS				
ABALONES	Blue-green Abalone	*Rough exterior: iridescent interior*	8 in (20 cm)	California
	Red Abalone	*Rough, red exterior: iridescent interior*	12 in (30 cm)	Philippines, S. California, N. Mexico
CHANK SHELLS	West Indian Chank	*Pointed apex: wide aperture*	10 in (25 cm)	Bahamas, Cuba, Mexico
CONCHS	Goliath Conch	*Rare: largest conch in the world*	14 in (35 cm)	Brazil
	Queen Conch	*Pale pink lip: very popular*	10 in (25 cm)	S. Florida, West Indies
FULGUR WHELKS	* Channelled Whelk	*Very large aperture*	6 in (15 cm)	East Coast, U.S.
	* Knobbed Whelk	*Very large pink aperture*	7 in (17·5 cm)	
	* Lightning Whelk	*Large aperture: elegant*	16 in (40 cm)	
HELMET SHELLS	Horned Helmet	*Off-white, shiny: golden interior*	8 in (20 cm)	W. Pacific Ocean depths
	King Helmet	*Triangular: beige, brown: teeth-like markings*	7 in (17·5 cm)	Indo-Pacific
MUREX SHELLS	* Ramose Murex	*Very beautiful: white branches, tinted pink*	12 in (30 cm)	Indo-Pacific
TRITONS	* Pacific Triton	*Dramatic shape: white/brown scalloped patterns*	14 in (35 cm)	Indo-Pacific
TULIP SHELLS	* Florida Horse Conch	*Huge: pointed apex: golden aperture: surface tends to flake*	20 in (50 cm)	Carolinas, U.S., Gulf of Mexico
	True Tulip	*Common: simple shape*	6 in (15 cm)	Carolinas, U.S., West Indies
TURBANS	* Green Turban	*Green exterior: wide pearl interior*	8 in (20 cm)	East Indies, Australia
VOLUTES	Ethiopian Volute	*Very wide aperture: honey coloured, darker bands*	14 in (35 cm)	Indo-Pacific
	Mammal Volute	*Wide aperture: brown scribbled markings on beige*	10 in (25 cm)	S. Australia

Group	Sub-species	Description	Maximum Size	Regions
2 BIVALVES				
COCKLES	Giant Heart Cockle	*Beautiful globular shape: pink, white: regular ribs*	5 in (12·5 cm)	E. Africa
	Costate Cockle	*Uncommon: white: knife-like ribs: deep interior*	6 in (15 cm)	W. Africa
PEARL OYSTERS	Black-Lip Pearl Oyster	*Pearly interior: dull silver exterior, black-edged*	6 in (15 cm)	S.E. Asia
	Gold Lip Pearl Oyster	*Iridescent pearly interior, gold at edges: buff exterior*	9 in (22·5 cm)	Philippines
SCALLOPS	Lion's Paw	*Usually cream, brown: rarely orange, yellow*	6 in (15 cm)	N. Carolina to Venezuela
	Noble Scallop	*Spectacular rainbow colours, mauve, yellow, orange: red very rare*	5 in (12·5 cm)	Japan
	Swift's Scallop	*Pretty rose, mauve colours: sometimes white, banded with pink*	5 in (12·5 cm)	Japan
THORNY OYSTERS	Eastern Thorny Oyster	*Magnificent spines: white, pink, red*	8 in (20 cm)	Gulf of Mexico
	Regal Thorny Oyster	*Uncommon: red, orange, purple*	8 in (20 cm)	S.E. Asia
3 CEPHALOPODS				
ARGONAUTS	Paper Nautilus	*Beautiful shape and textured surface: deep interior: delicate*	12 in (30 cm)	Warm seas
NAUTILUS	Chambered Nautilus	*Famous shell: very deep interior: brown markings on off-white*	8 in (20 cm)	W. Pacific ocean depths

All those shells marked with an asterisk are very suitable for planting with seeds, small
bulbs or cuttings, as they have wide apertures and are extremely strong. The Paper
Nautilus and the Chambered Nautilus are both wide enough, but are delicate, particularly
the former, and need very careful handling. When choosing plants either for the garden
or the house, make sure that their proportions are in keeping with their shell containers.
It would look quite odd to have a comparatively small shell sprouting immensely long
fronds. Equally, shapes of leaves and flowers should complement the shells and not over-
whelm them; compact, bushy, trailing or creeping plants look lovely (*see photograph 47*)
but those with erect growing habits can look strange and stiff.
I have listed a few plants for your consideration, together with brief descriptions, preferred
positions and average sizes.

46

SHELLS AND FLOWERS

Type	Name	Situation	Description	Average Size
ALPINES	Cinquefoil (Shrubby varieties)	Sun	Yellow, orange flowers	6 in (15 cm)
	Edelweiss	Sun	Blue, white flowers	6 in (15 cm)
	Navelwort	Shade	Trailing blue flowers	10 in (25 cm)
	Saxifragia	Shade	Dense yellow flowers	4 in (10 cm)
	Soapwort	Sun	Trailing pink flowers	14 in (35 cm)
ANNUALS	Lobelia	Sun or partial shade	Usually blue, white flowers	Compact 4 in (10 cm) Trailing 12 in (30 cm)
	Ivy-leaved Pelargonium	Sun	Pink, red, white, mauve flowers: trailing	12 in (30 cm)
	Nasturtium	Sun or partial shade	Yellow, orange flowers: plant in poor soil	Dwarf 4 in (10 cm) Trailing 12 in (30 cm)
BIENNIALS	Dwarf Campanula	Sun or partial shade	Blue-mauve flowers	4 in (10 cm)
	Forget-me-not	Sun or partial shade	Tiny blue flowers	6 in (15 cm)
BULBS	Dwarf Crocus	In or out of doors	White, yellow, blue, mauve, purple flowers	4 in (10 cm)
	Winter Aconite	Partial shade or open position	Yellow flowers	4 in (10 cm)
FRAGRANT PLANTS	Artemisia	Sun	Silver rock plant	6 in (15 cm)
	Dwarf Lavender	Sun	White, mauve flowers	6 in (15 cm)
	Pennyroyal	Sun	Peppermint scent	Prostrate
	Rock Hyssop	Sun	Deep blue flowers	10 in (25 cm)
	Thrift	Sun	Deep pink flowers	8 in (20 cm)
HEATHERS	Dwarf varieties	Sun	Evergreen: white, pink, mauve flowers	10 in (25 cm)
HERBS	Aniseed	Sun	Seeds flavour cakes: leaves for salads	Low-growing
	Chives	Partial shade	Subtle onion flavour for salads, omelettes	6 in (15 cm)
	Marjoram	Sun	Flavours meats, salads	12 in (30 cm)
	Tarragon	Sun	Flavours chicken, salads	12 in (30 cm)
	Thyme	Sun	Savoury stuffings, meat	12 in (30 cm)

HOUSE PLANTS (see colour photograph and photographs 45 and 47).

Type	Name	Situation	Description	Comments
FLOWERING	African Violet	Light, but out of direct sun	Compact: pink, white, mauve, purple flowers	Difficult: needs moisture, freedom from draughts and changes of temperature
	Impatiens (Busy Lizzie)	Sun	Profuse, bushy, quick-growing: red, white, pink flowers	Easy: needs plenty of water in summer, little in winter

Type	Name	Situation	Description	Comments
NON-FLOWERING	Chlorophytum	Light	*Striped green/white leaves, young plants borne on end of arched stems*	Easy: keep moist
	Helxine	Anywhere, but thrives in partial shade	*Small, creeping: bright green leaves*	Easy: keep moist always
	Ivy	Light, avoid direct sun	*Many forms: mostly green, variegated: trailing*	Easy: keep moist, do not over-water
	Maidenhair Fern	Light: out of direct sun	*Delicate pale green leaves in sprays*	Difficult: water frequently, keep away from draughts
	Rhoicissus	Shady	*Creeping: dark green leaves, abundant*	Easy: keep slightly moist
	Tradescantia	Light	*Trailing or creeping: usually small, striped leaves*	Easy: grow in poor soil: keep slightly moist
CACTI (C) AND SUCCULENTS (S)	Echeveria derenbergii (S)	Light, sunny: can be put out of doors May–September	*Compact, rosette formation: reddish-yellow flowers*	Water freely April–September. Reduce moisture October–November. Leave unwatered December–January. Light watering February–March
	Euphorbia meloformis (S)	Light, sunny: can be put out of doors May–September	*Globular: tiny green flowers*	Water freely April–September. Reduce moisture October–November. Leave unwatered December–January. Light watering February–March
	Mammilaria bombycina (C)	Light, sunny: can be put out of doors May–September	*Rings of red flowers: globular later elongated*	Water freely April–September. Reduce moisture October–November. Leave unwatered December–January. Light watering February–March
	Pachyphytum oviferum (S) (the sugar almond plant)	Light, sunny: can be put out of doors May–September	*Tiny, shrub-like: small fat leaves, tinged pink*	As above, but take care not to water or touch leaves, as the bloom rubs off easily
	Rebutia (C)	Light, sunny: can be put out of doors May–September	*Compact: very free-flowering*	As first three listed

FRESH FLOWERS

The colour photograph and *photograph 48* show how any shell that can hold as much as a spoonful of water can be used as a container. Miniature arrangements of single blooms look delightful in smaller shells, which can be kept horizontal by means of support underneath, using Plasticine or Blu-Tack. Flowers can be held in position by inserting their stalks in florists' foam or Oasis, which should first have been thoroughly soaked for about an hour.

DRIED FLOWERS

Dried and preserved flowers, leaves and grasses can be seen in *photograph 49*. They are long-lasting and with their subtle – often bleached – colours suit shells admirably. No water is needed – only a firm base made of polystyrene foam cut to size and fitted inside the container to hold the stalks in place. Plasticine makes a good alternative holding material and has the advantage of being usable over and over again.

Shells with house plants

On the bottom shelf in the colour photograph is a pink-flowered African Violet planted in a Giant Cockle, next to a finely-beaded member of the Frog Shell family, the *Ranella girina*, complete with a succulent and its offshoots. Two Triton Trumpets are on the second shelf – the larger has Tradescantia, ivy and a fern while the smaller contains an Impatiens. A white Campanula in a Green Turban is on the top shelf.

Shells with fresh flowers

The colour photograph shows a beige and white banded shell, known appropriately enough as the Banded Tun Shell; to the left, with cherries (real, not wax ones!) is a Coral Snail. The rose in the centre is in a Turban and above, on the left, is a Ramose Murex. The shell on the top right of the picture is a simple Great Scallop valve.

49   *50*

Containers for Shells

Shells, instead of containing something, may themselves be contained in something else.
Glass jars with stoppers or lids are the best way of showing them off and protecting them
at the same time, as can be seen in *photograph 50*. A mixture of small, colourful shells looks
like a jar of candy, particularly if the shells are of shiny varieties. Using shells of all one
colour or sub-species looks very effective, too. A pair of long tweezers is extremely useful
for lowering them into place or for removing them if wrongly placed. Interesting pebbles,
either in their natural state or polished in a stone-polishing tumbler, are even simpler to
arrange – just drop them in.

CHAPTER 8
THINGS TO MAKE
AND DECORATE

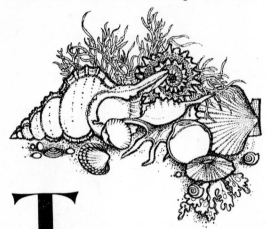

Through the ages shells have been used for many unlikely articles. Ingenuity led people to use Windowpane Oysters for screens, windows, lamps and even roofs, to cut cameos from Helmet Shells and to make kitchen utensils from Scallop Shells. Shells have been used extensively to decorate useful objects, particularly in Victorian times, while rows of Cowries are used to adorn the prows of fishing boats in the Pacific Ocean. To take it one step further still: objects made from shells – pearl buttons – are sewn to clothes to make the world-famous London Costermongers' Pearly King and Queen costumes.

DECORATIVE OBJECTS

Fish server and ladle

Implements like those in *photograph 51*, often with carved bamboo handles, used to be made by Pacific Islanders. This idea can be easily adapted to simpler methods – in this case, bamboo wound tightly with string. Scallop Shells may be obtained from most fishmongers, particularly in season.

You will need

1 Great Scallop (convex and flat valves)
Two lengths of bamboo each about 10 in (25 cm) long
Sharp knife
Strong adhesive
Two small lengths of wire about 6 in (15 cm) long
Two lengths of thin cane each about 30 in (75 cm) long
Ball of string
Bodkin or safety-pin

Method   Cut one piece of bamboo to the length required and carve two notches either side of one end for the Scallop to fit into (*see diagram Ja*), using the knife as if sharpening a pencil. When the notches are the right size to fit the flat top of the shell, secure the two together with adhesive, and twist the wire round at the base two or three times, over the notches, to ensure a firm grip (*see diagram Jb*).

Next, make two very small splits at the top of the bamboo on either side, directly above the notches at the base. (These are made in order to secure the handle to the bamboo.) To make the handle, take one length of cane or thick garden wire and coil it four times into a circle measuring about $2\frac{1}{2}$ in (6 cm) in diameter, leaving a short bit of about 1 in (25 mm) to fit into the top of the bamboo. Now take a long piece of string, measuring about 2 yds (2 m), and thread the end through a bodkin or safety-pin. Leaving the short end of the cane free, wind the string tightly over the cane all the way round (*see diagram Jc*).

Keeping hold of the remaining string, insert the free end of the cane circle in to the hollow at the top of the bamboo, and pull the string *down* in to one of the splits that you have made. Take the string across, and pull it *up* through the other split. Pass the bodkin through the

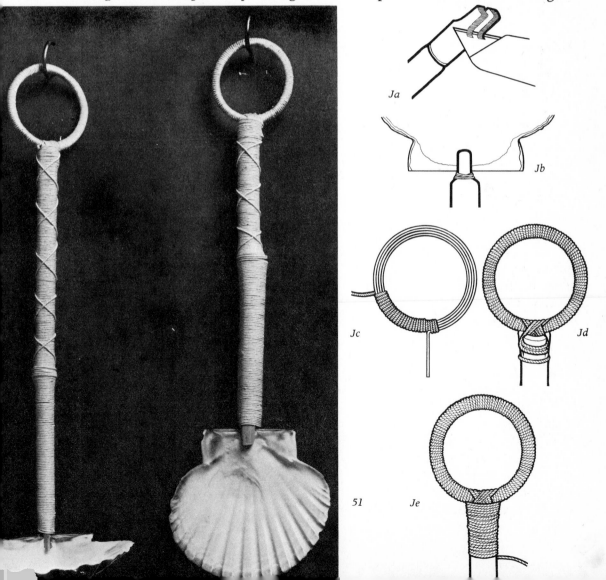

Ja

Jb

Jc

Jd

51   Je

circle, and repeat this process several times, back and front, until you are satisfied that it is quite secure (*see diagram Jd*). Join the remainder of the string to the end of the whole ball of string, using a reef knot at the back of the handle, and wind it very tightly down the bamboo (*see diagram Je*). Fasten off at the base, using some adhesive as well as a knot, for extra security. Make criss-cross or diagonal patterns if you wish to. These implements, besides looking decorative, are also functional, provided that care is taken to fix the three separate parts firmly together.

SHELL SCULPTURE   This type of design seen in *colour photograph* and *photograph 52*, can be either purely decorative or decorative and functional at the same time. If the latter, the shells can act as receptacles for jewelry, make-up, sewing equipment, bric-à-brac, soap or any other small objects. The large shells are valves of a Furbelow Clam, perched either end of a weather-beaten piece of oak, probably once part of a wooden arch or door. The odd-looking clump fixed to the interior of the valve on the right is a Worm Shell, and the mushroom-like disc on the opposite side is, in fact, known as a Mushroom Coral. Pieces of driftwood, particularly those with unusual shapes, can be useful in this context, giving an unexpected, slightly surrealist, look to ordinary objects.

MINIATURE FURNITURE   seen in *photograph 53*. These are for children to make, using bits and pieces that can be found in most homes.

You will need

CHEST-OF-DRAWERS
6 empty matchboxes
Patterned or coloured paper
6 rounded shells for drawer knobs
4 flat-bottomed shells (optional)
Light adhesive
Strong adhesive
Scissors

CHAIR
2 Scallop valves
1 large bell cap (*see Chapter 6*)
1 empty spool of thread
Felt to cover top and sides of the spool
Light adhesive
Strong adhesive
Scissors

MIRROR
1 Scallop valve
1 obsolete silver coin
1 small shell to support mirror
Strong adhesive

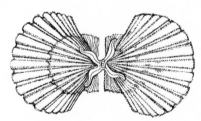

Method

CHEST-OF-DRAWERS   Spread the strong adhesive over one side each of two matchboxes, and stick them together side by side. Repeat this with the remaining two pairs. When they are dry, glue the top surface of one pair and place another pair on top, making sure that all the sides are level. Then do the same with the third pair.

When the chest-of-drawers is quite dry, lay it on your chosen paper and draw, first, round the top, then down the two sides, and lastly, round the front of each drawer. You can, of course, cover the sides of the drawers too, if you like, but unless you use very thin paper, this may make them rather a tight fit. Cut the pieces out carefully, and stick them in place using the light adhesive. This will take about quarter of an hour to dry sufficiently to be

52

53

able to add the shell 'knobs' (Periwinkles in this case) to each of the drawers, having first placed the chest horizontally. When they in turn are dry, add a flat-bottomed shell to each of the four corners at the base to make the feet; Nerites were used for the chest in the picture.

MIRROR   Simply fix the coin to the interior of the Scallop shell with strong adhesive and, when it is dry, stick a small, strong shell to the back to support it.

CHAIR   Lay the two valves of the Scallop, outside facing you, on a flat surface with their straight ends facing each other and almost touching. Take the bell cap and put a generous amount of strong adhesive under it. Place it on the shells in the position shown in *diagram K*. While you are waiting for it to dry, cut two pieces of felt to cover the top and sides of the spool. For the top, stand the spool on the felt and draw round it using a pencil or a felt-tipped pen if it is dark material; for the sides, measure the height and circumference with a piece of string, and draw the required strip on the felt with the help of a ruler. Cut the two pieces out and stick them on to the spool using the light adhesive. Lastly, when the shells have set, gently bend the two valves towards each other, until they are almost at right angles; the bell cap acts as a sort of hinge. Glue the flatter Scallop on to the top of the spool, using the strong adhesive; and weight it with a stone or similar object, while it is setting.

DECORATIVE OBJECTS

When fixing shells with adhesive to the surfaces of three-dimensional objects, the work should be done horizontally. If an attempt is made to work vertically, the shells will merely slide down, unless they are individually held in position with Blu-Tack. In exceptional circumstances when continual change of position might result in damage to a delicate object like a clock, working vertically may be necessary. However, most boxes, table surfaces and so on present no such problems. It follows that each surface must be done separately and allowed to set before starting on the next one. When there are no more shell-less areas for the object to rest on but there are still one or two sides to complete, a folded-up towel or small pillow placed underneath will prevent the shells breaking. They are surprisingly strong and providing you proceed with reasonable care, they will stand up to this treatment.

TWO ROUND BOXES   Only the tops of the boxes shown in *colour photograph* and *photograph 54* have been decorated and they are very straightforward to make. Small shells suit small areas rather better than larger ones, but they can be difficult to pick up and put in position, so you will almost certainly need a pair of fine tweezers. Shells of one variety can be bought in small bags in some specialist shops or, of course, collected on the seashore. The larger of the two boxes has a smooth pebble surmounted by a crusty-looking Periwinkle as its central lifting device and it is surrounded by Dog Whelks, Rose Petal Tellins and Pearly Trochuses. A pale pink, egg-shaped pebble makes an equally firm knob in the middle of the second box and radiating outwards are Ceriths, Margin Shells (these are known as Coffee Beans), Rose Petal Tellins and Rice Shells, which are members of the Olive family.

GOBLET   Originally a wooden egg-cup (and hardly usable for that purpose any more), the curves of this goblet seen in *colour photograph* and *photograph 55* made it difficult to cover more than a very small area at a time. For working purposes it is best to lay **any**

54 awkwardly shaped object like this on its side in a sort of bed made out of Plasticine or

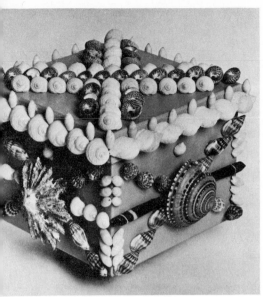

56   57

Blu-Tack and decorate only that area which has the least slope. Each part must be dry before the next bit is done, and so on. Small shells with flattish bases, like the tiny Limpets, Periwinkles and white Olive Shells used here, adapt much more easily to rounded surfaces than do large ones.

SQUARE BOX   The lid and sides of the bright red cardboard box seen in *photograph 56* were decorated with strong shells, so that when the last two sides had to be worked on horizontally, the shells underneath were in no danger of being crushed. Four fine-looking shells – two Common Atlantic Sundials and two Star Limpets – were placed centrally on each of the sides; these were fixed vertically, and kept in position with Blu-Tack while they were setting. The white Whelks are, in fact, Banded Whelks (no bands on these though, for some reason) and the slim white shells are Olives. Dog Whelks and Top Shells, pearly apertures facing upwards, were also used to make the diagonal lines.

CLOCK   Pearl buttons, one of the best-known products made from shells, are expensive these days, and can be difficult to find in this age of plastics. I was lucky enough to have had quite a lot for some time, and the idea of mingling shells and objects *made* out of shells appealed to me. The clock seen in *colour photograph* and *photograph 57* was bought cheaply in a junk shop, where it had, apparently, been sitting in a corner for years. Instead of using pearl buttons, Pearly Trochuses, relatives of the Commercial Trochus used for button-making, would look lovely; indeed, any small regularly-shaped shells could be used to make a background for larger shells. At the top is a Vase Shell behind an orange Moon Snail and in front of a Turritella. To either side are members of the Cockle family, square-edged, for which there is no colloquial English name. Their Latin name is *Cardium unedo*. Near the bottom of the clock are two Wing Oysters, in between which are Limpets, Cockles, land Snails and a single Moon Snail.

Conclusion

Collecting shells and using them creatively is a most rewarding occupation and I hope that the information and ideas contained in this book will lead to many hours of pleasure and maybe even a lifelong interest.

It should be explained that just a few shells have more than one colloquial English name and in such cases I have chosen to use the best-known one. Some shells also appear in the text under official Latin names; this is because no known English equivalents exist.

Finally, I would like to thank two people very much for their invaluable help: Mrs Avril Rodway, who acted in an advisory capacity and Kenneth Wye of Eaton's, Manette Street, London W.1 who helped to identify many of the shells.

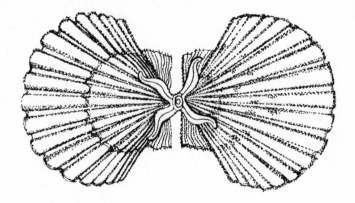

Common and Latin Names of Shells

ABALONE Haliotis
AMERICAN WHELK-TINGLE Urosalpinx cinerea
ARABIAN COWRIE Cypraea arabicula
Arca anadara
ARGONAUT Argonauta
ARK SHELL Arca
ATLANTIC BUBBLE Bulla striata
ATLANTIC DEEP SEA SCALLOP Placopecten
  magellanicus
AUGER Terebra
AUGER TURRITELLA Turritella terebra
AUSTRALIAN TOP SHELL Trochus niloticus
AUSTRALIAN TRUMPET Syrinx aruana
BANDED TUN SHELL Tonna sulcosa
BANDED WHELK Nucella lapillus
BLACK LIP PEARL OYSTER Pinctada margaritifera
BLOOD COWRIE Cypraea carneola
BUBBLE SHELL Bulla
BULL MOUTH HELMET Cypraecassis rufa
Bullia
CALICO CLAM Macrocallista maculata
CARDITA Cardita
Cardium unedo
CARRIER SHELLS Xenophora
CEPHALOPOD Cephalopoda
CERITH Cerithium
CHAMBERED NAUTILUS Nautilus pompilius
CHANK Turbinella
CHANNELLED BABYLON Babylonia canaliculata
CHANNELLED WHELK Busycon canaliculatum
CHINA LIMPET Patella aspera
CHINAMAN'S HAT Calyptraea mamillaris
CHINK SHELL Lacuna
CHITON Chiton
CLAM
CLUB URCHIN SPINES
COAT-OF-MAIL SHELL Chiton
COCKLE Cardium
COFFEE BEAN Marginella
COMB SHELL Glycymeris glycymeris
COMMERCIAL TROCHUS Trochus niloticus
COMMON ATLANTIC SUNDIAL Architectonica
  nobilis
COMMON COCKLE Cerastoderma edule
COMMON HAIRY TRITON Cymatium pileare
COMMON LIMPET Patella vulgata
COMMON MUSSEL Mytilus edulis
CONCH Strombus
CONE Conus

CORAL
CORAL SNAIL Rapa
COSTATE COCKLE Cardium costatum
COWRIE Cyprea
CROWN CONCH Melangena corona
CUTTLE-BONE
CUTTLEFISH Sepia officinalis
Cymatium caudatum
DATE MUSSEL
DIMIDIATE AUGER Terebra dimidiata
DOG WHELK Nucella lapillus
DOVE SHELL Pyrene
DYE MUREX Murex brandaris
EASTERN THORNY OYSTER Spondylus americanus
EGG COWRIES Cypraeacea
EMERALD NERITE Smaragdis viridis
ETHIOPIAN VOLUTE Melo aethiopicus
EUROPEAN COWRIE Cypraea europaea
FESTIVAL SNAIL Plotia terebellum
FIG SHELLS Tonnacea
FLAT WINKLE Littorina littorea
FLORIDA HORSE CONCH Pleuroploca gigantea
FLUTED GIANT CLAM Tridacna squamosa
FROG SHELL Bursa
FULGUR WHELK Busycon
FURBELOW CLAM Tridacna squamosa
GAPER Mya
GEOGRAPHY CONE Conus geographus
GIANT CLAM Tridacnida gigas
GIANT COCKLE Cardium lima
GIANT HEART COCKLE
GIANT SUNDIAL Architectonica maxima
GIRDLED ROCK SHELL Thais cingulata
GLORY-OF-THE-SEA CONE Conus gloria-maris
GOLD LIP PEARL OYSTER
GOLIATH CONCH Strombus goliath
GREAT SCALLOP Pecten maximus
GREEN TURBAN Turbo marmoratus
HARD-SHELL CLAM Venus mercenaria
HARP Harpa
HEART COCKLE Corculum cardissa
HELMET SHELL Cassis
HORNED HELMET Cassis cornuta
JAPANESE CARRIER SHELL Xenophora pallidula
JINGLE SHELL Anomia ephippium
JOB'S TEAR Donax
KEYHOLE LIMPET Fissurella
KING HELMET Cassis tuberosa
KNOBBED WHELK Busycon carica

LADY'S EAR Sinum
LAND SNAILS Cerionidae
        Helicidae
LATIAXIS SHELL Latiaxis
LEOPARD SCALLOP Annachlamys leopardus
LEUCODON COWRIE Cypraea leucodon
LIGHTNING WHELK Busycon contrarium
LIMPET Acmaea
LION'S PAW SCALLOP Lyropecten nodosus
Lischkiea alwinae
LITTLE BOX DOG WHELK Nassarius arcularis
LITTLE EGG COWRIE Calpurnus verrucosus
LUCINES Lucinidae
LYNX COWRIE Cypraea lynx
LYRATE COCKLE Discors lyrata
MAGNIFICENT WENTLETRAP Amaea magnifica
MAMMAL VOLUTE Livonia mammilla
MANTLE SCALLOP Pecten pallium
MARBLE CONE Conus marmareus
MARGIN SHELL Marginella
MARLINSPIKE AUGER Terebra maculata
MITRE Mitra
MONEY COWRIE Cypraea moneta
MONOPLACOPHORA Monoplacophora
MOON SNAIL Natica
MOUSE COWRIE Cypraea mus
MUREX SHELL Murex
Murex trapa
MUSHROOM CORAL
MUSSEL Mytilus
Natica mamilla
NAUTILUS Nautilus
NECKLACE SHELLS Naticacea
NERITE Nerita
NETTED DOG WHELK Nassa reticulata
NOBLE PEN SHELL Pinna nobilis
NOBLE SCALLOP Chlamys nobilis
NODOSE PAPER NAUTILUS Argonauta nodosa
NUCLEUS COWRIE Cypraea nucleus
Oliva reticularis nivosa
OLIVANCILLARIA Olivancillaria
OLIVE Oliva
ORMER Haliotis tuberculata
OTTER SHELL Lutratia
OWL LIMPET Lottia gigantea
OYSTER Mytilus
PACIFIC TRITON Charonia tritonis
PAINTED TOP SHELL Calliostoma amabilis
PAPAL MITRE Mitra papalis
PAPER NAUTILUS Argonauta argo
Patella miniata
PEARL OYSTERS Pteriacea
PEARLY FRESH WATER MUSSELS Unionidae
PEARLY NAUTILUS Nautilus pompilius
PEARLY TROCHUS Calliostoma occidentale
Pecten flabellum
PELICAN'S FOOT Aporrhais pes-pelicani
PEN SHELL Pinna
PERIWINKLE Littorina littorea
PHEASANT SHELL Phasianella
PIDDOCK Pholas
POACHED EGG COWRIE Ovula ovum
POND SNAIL
PRECIOUS WENTLETRAP Epitonium scalare
PRICKLY FROG SHELL Bursa rana
PURPLE DRUPE Drupa morum

PYRENE Columbella
QUEEN CONCH Strombus gigas
RAMOSE MUREX Murex ramosus
Ranella girina
RAZOR SHELLS Solenacea
RED ABALONE Haliotis rufescens
REGAL THORNY OYSTER Spondylus regius
RICE SHELL Oliva
ROCK SHELL Thais
ROSE PETAL TELLIN Tellina lineata
ROTARY STAR SHELL Astraea rotularia
ROUGH WINKLE Littorina saxatilis
SADDLE OYSTER Anomia ephippium
SCALLOP Pecten
SCREW SHELL Turritella communis
SHIPWORM Teredo
SLIPPER SHELL Crepidula
SLIT SHELL Pleurotomaria
SNIPE'S BILL MUREX Murex haystellum
SPIKED LIMPET Patella longicosta
SPINDLE TIBIA Tibia fusus
SPINY COCKLE Cardium aculeatum
SQUID Loligo forbesii
SQUILLA CLAW
STAR LIMPET Patella astra
STAR SHELL Astraea
SUNDIAL Architectonica
SURF CLAM Mactra
SWIFT'S SCALLOP Chlamys swifti
Tapes turgida
TAPESTRY TURBAN Turbo petholatus
Tectarius muricatus
TELLIN Tellina
Tellina albinella
TEXTILE CONE Conus textile
THORNY OYSTERS Spondylidae
THRUSH COWRIE Cypraea turdus
TOP SHELL Trochus
TRITON Charonia
TRITON TRUMPET Charonia
Tritonidea undosus
TRIUMPHANT STAR Guildfordia triumphans
TRUE LIMPETS Acmaeidae
TULIP SHELL Fasciolaria
TUN SHELL Tonna
TURBAN Turbo
TURRID Turris
TURRITELLA Turritella
TUSK SHELL Dentalium
UNSTABLE LIMPET Acmaea instabilis
VASE SHELL Vasum
VENUS CLAMS Veneridae
VIBEX BONNET Casmaria erinaceus
VIOLET SNAIL Janthina
VOLUTE Voluta
WANDERING COWRIE Cypraea errones
WEDGE SHELL Donax
WENTLETRAP Epitonium
WEST INDIAN CHANK SHELL Turbinella angulata
WHELK Buccinum undatum
WHITE BANDED BUBBLE Hydatina albocincta
WINDOWPANE OYSTER Placuna placenta
WING OYSTER Pteria
WINKLE Littorina littorea
WORM SHELLS Vermetidae
ZEBRA ARK SHELL Arca zebra